Flowers in the Frost

Praise for Flowers in the Frost

What my community members think

"I couldn't put it down yesterday - the structure "personal story - thoughtful further exploration" got me hooked and I just wanted to read the next chapter. Genius. I read the last chapters at a cozy little café I've just discovered, on a date with myself for the first time in ages. I've enjoyed your book tremendously, every word speaks to me... I'll get back to it again and again for sure."

Danae Florou, Alpha Beta Greek

"OMG, I am LOVING reading about you and your personal story. I just made it to the middle of the first chapter, but I'm already hooked."

Inés Ramos, Portraits of Spain

"At the end of chapter 3 now, and so many ideas and inspiration are blossoming in my head. I already know my paperback copy will be filled with notes on the sides, little doodles, plenty of highlighted sentences..."

Elena Gabrielli, Hitoritabi Languages

"I have just read the whole book. But because I was so inspired and read it all in almost one sitting, I'm going to go back and read it all over again! There's so much there that gave me an "a-ha" moment, but one quote stands out: "Share your vision - not your tips". It's fabulous inspiration!"

Clare Whitmell, English at Home

"I'll get back to your book at different stages of my online business. Thank you for your encouraging words. By the way, my favorite quote is that of Antoine De Saint-Exupéry!"

Alexandra Kapinya, Visual English School

"Elena's latest book is just the thing if you've been working on your dream for what seems like a long time now and you want to find the motivation, the hope and the new strategies you need as you continue to grow as an entrepreneur."

Trisha Traughber, Vagabond English

The Untold Stories
OF ONLINE TEACHING

by Elena Mutonono

Dedication

To all the language teachers out there who had the courage to take their work online, to be exposed and vulnerable. You help people travel, discover the multifaceted world of vibrant cultures, get settled in new countries, and find joy in life through learning languages.

Your work matters.

You might feel like you're sowing flowers in the frost, but I believe that your passion will one day melt the snow, and you will see the fruit of your labor. I pray that you do not grow weary, that you find inspiration and courage to make a difference in the lives of those you seek to impact.

I hope that you stay connected, hydrated and focused — you need your strength to run this marathon. Keep going. Don't stop halfway. One day you will know that your efforts have not been in vain.

On this poor, indigent ground
I shall sow flowers of flowing colors;
I shall sow flowers even amidst the frost,
And water them with my bitter tears.

And from those burning tears will melt
The frozen crust, so hard and strong,
Perhaps the flowers will bloom and
Bring about for me a joyous spring.

— "Contra Spem Spero,"
by Lesya Ukrainka

Contents

Introduction

"Because there is only one of you in all of time, the expression is unique. And if you block it, it will never exist through any other medium and it will be lost."

— *Kathryn Craft*

THE YEAR OF LOSING EVERYTHING and gaining everything... That's what 2014 was like for me, my personal life and my business. The losing part is devastating. It's like running into the cool Black Sea in the summer, thinking of swimming and fun and then suddenly slipping, falling into the water and trying to cry for help. You open your mouth, but only bubbles come out. The seconds in the water feel like long, drawn-out desperation.

In March 2014, I lost my homeland. My gorgeous Crimea with its summer aromas of the salty sea, cypress trees and pines became someone else's land. I watched all this from another country, thousands of miles away, wishing a new piece of news would somehow change what was happening, revert the flood and stop this madness.

Each month the avalanche of changes rolled on, threatening to bury everything I had created. At the time I'd been teaching online for four years, with a steady stream of clients, several teachers working for me and no cash flow problems. Time, of course, was an issue, and I had no idea how to "grow" that thing, but at least it was doing well for a one-person gig.

By the end of the year I'd lost 90% of my clients, let my teachers go and was left behind trying to pick up the pieces of a business that had been in the red for over six months. I wanted to turn it around. I needed to turn it around, but how? Nothing I'd learned before 2014 had taught me how to deal with something like that. It's the helplessness you feel when you lose control and can't regain it. So looking for real help, outside of Google or YouTube, was the only thing I knew would help me figure things out.

For the first four years, I'd stuck with the same strategy of linear growth: If I wanted to grow my 1-on-1 business I had to have more clients. If I maxed out all of my time, I had to hire more people, train them, pay them and pocket the rest.

Managing several teachers had been overwhelming, and I had no idea what I would do if I recruited more students. That's what everyone in my industry was thinking and doing, at least those giving private lessons. Creating online courses seemed like a good possibility, but selling them "wasn't my thing," so I was stuck.

Being in the red for six months snapped me back to reality. I had to learn about growth in a different way. I had to know where I'd gone "wrong," and what I could do differently. Reflecting on my business, some of the lessons stood out to me. I had thought my "niche" was the people living in the Russian-speaking countries. I'd offered too many services and I'd been afraid of offering them to anyone outside of my familiar circles. Looking back, I wonder why anyone would want to focus on a geographical location when they teach online?

Seeing mistakes, though, doesn't help find a solution that works. I lacked the confidence to create my own action plan. Later, I remember going through the materials of a business course, and one thought struck me. The author said, "If you want to grow your business, the first and most common technique is to add more clients. But that's on the surface level. Instead of that, you can change what you offer."

Those words went off like a lightning bolt in my consciousness. It meant that I didn't need to add more teachers or more administrators to new teachers. It meant that I could spend less time managing other employees, and more time helping clients achieve their goals. It meant that I could (at least try to) work smarter, not harder.

In 2014, I discovered that losing everything could mean two things: complete defeat or a new beginning.

This book is my journey from a painful loss into the world of working smarter, creating more "white space" for my passions and more freedom for the life I've wanted — a life of growth, creativity and curiosity. In this book I will talk about overcoming impostor syndrome, impacting people all over the world, and challenging myself to make meaning doing what I loved.

Each chapter will start with a real-life story, and then I will talk more about the technical steps and mindset shifts necessary to achieve the dream of working less and accomplishing more. You will also hear some of my clients' stories, to prove that your dream isn't just a figment of imagination, and that anyone with a desire to challenge the status quo can do the impossible.

CHAPTER 1.
Building a Business in the Face of Moral Injuries

THE CRISP CRIMEAN MORNING AIR in early June spoiled me with its coolness until the sun hung high, revealing pillars of dust rising from sloppily paved sidewalks, making the air hot, dry and stifling. I was sitting at the old desk in my classroom, all four windows open, enjoying the quiet as the school was no longer in session. Expecting only one student to show up for my office hours, I began planning what I'd do after work. The thought of grocery shopping before the working crowds hit every supermarket made me feel powerful, important and free.

The student cracked the door open and told me she was ready with her questions. She walked in wearing heels, a miniskirt and a cheerful, almost childish smile. She was one of the students I never could figure out. Socially awkward, Sasha* never mingled with others much. She wore odd clothes and communicated by yelling whenever she got excited. She was in her first year of college living outside her tiny, endearing Rybachye village. I believe the entire village must have been proud of her for going to college. Yet, Sasha had a few learning disabilities and social issues that made progress slow. So she took every chance she had to improve before the tests whacked her out of balance.

I opened the textbook and we began going over some boring grammar stuff that students always struggled with, but the school forced them to learn. As she was getting ready to leave I got up to encourage her to keep working hard or some other banality we used to say to students that weren't linguistically inclined (about 50% of all of the people I had taught at a college that was "supposed" to train linguists). She pulled out a piece of paper and gave it to me.

I looked down. Shocked. Humiliated. Ambushed.

I heard my own heartbeat as though someone had amplified it right in my ears.

Money. A note with roughly a quarter of my meager Ukrainian College salary. The portrait of a Ukrainian civil and political activist, who spoke justice and freedom, Lesya Ukrainka, looked at me from the note. I cringed. I couldn't believe someone had just offered me a bribe. I felt violated and somehow dirty, although bribing teachers must have seemed normal for a girl from a village school.

Fumbling for words, I opened the door to get her out of the room, pushing the note into her hands. She threw it back at me and ran away. I picked up the "Lesya Ukrainka" wondering what to do next.

. . .

*"On this poor, indigent ground
I shall sow flowers of flowing colors;
I shall sow flowers even amidst the frost,
And water them with my bitter tears."*

— *Lesya Ukrainka*

We've all had similar stories where teaching at a school challenged not just our mental state, but our moral compass. I had never thought anyone would offer me a bribe. I'd always seen those bribe-loving professors as those who compromised once, found an excuse and then justified the process as something "normal" and ordinary.

Bribes were rampant when I was a student and later when I became a college professor in Ukraine. I walked away from my Ph.D. program when I discovered that the only way to get the coveted diploma was by "feeding the supervisor." The other two options, as I was told, to get a Ph.D. in Applied Linguistics in Ukraine were to sleep with the professor or to have mighty connections.

Sometimes there was no way around bribing because corruption ran deep, but me? Offered a bribe? I was not a Ph.D. and had been expressing my opinions on corruption every time I got on the soapbox, so this surprised me and pained me at the same time.

When I switched to teaching online I felt compelled to create a little world of justice, fairness and worth. I wanted to treat others fairly and charge what I felt I deserved.

I didn't want to be told why a student I'd never seen had to get a grade anyway and who his dad was and how that impacted my professional life. Yet until I "opted out" from that classroom, I'd never thought working for myself was something that might help solve this dilemma.

What I found ironic at the beginning of my online teaching journey was that the plagues I'd left at the college when it shut down followed me into my online business. I still tolerated pesty clients, underpaid myself and treated myself like a slave by working more hours and having no life. I believed I had to go through this stoically though, because it was a part of the deal.

Even with the years, the injustices never went away until I made a conscious decision not to tolerate them. After all, if *I* didn't put a stop to these problems in my business, *who would do it for me?* Who would make sure I was treated fairly? Who would take care of my salary, my benefits and my retirement? Who would weed out poor-fit clients? Why would I continue victimizing myself? There were no demanding supervisors telling me what to do anymore.

I discovered years later that I'd suffered from a number of moral injuries that wouldn't go away on their own. Moral injuries are any experiences that "transgress deeply held moral beliefs and expectations." I realized that many teachers go through life with numerous moral injuries that make them feel unappreciated, violated and often humiliated. It's those times when they are forced to give a poor student a passing grade, close their eyes on cheating, collaborate with dysfunctional supervisors who demand bribes and favors, witness copyright infringement and other criminal violations and let them go.

What victims tend to do is to recreate this unfairness cycle everywhere they go. Just like victims of physical or sexual abuse who can't build healthy relationships until they deal with the root of the problem, few teachers are able to face their moral injuries and traumas, forgive, heal and move on.

So what did I do that helped me overcome the injuries before my business began to thrive? There is no progression or suggested order of these practices, but I believe we need to do all of them if we want to deal with our past and build a healthy future.

1. Cultivate mindfulness

Keeping a journal, practicing yoga, meditating, praying, doodling, drawing — these activities help us be more in control of our lives, not just react to whatever happens to us. There is a difference when you say, "It's impossible to find a high-paying client, I have bills to pay, and nobody wants to pay me what I need, so I'll just be doing that until something happens," and "I know I have responsibilities to take care of, and working with this person is a temporary thing while I'm building my business and make sure I only work with the people who are my loyal fans."

In the first scenario, we react to what life throws our way without reflecting on **what we can do to change it.** We accept it and become a victim. In the second case,

we are in control, and we realize that our situation is going to change as we are making efforts daily for that to happen. Keeping a journal as a part of a mindfulness routine helps us see things in perspective and be more in control.

2. Draft your manifesto

What are your values? What do you believe great work should be like? How can your values and practices work together? Many teachers feel it's futile to list their values since "practicing them is *never* going to happen." But when **we don't spell out what our ideal work is like**, it's hard to create it for ourselves in our business. At best, we'll be recreating our previous workplace; the past ridden with injuries and trauma.

A manifesto is a public declaration of the values that guide your work. Without it, we can't build the future we wish to see. We cannot make the change we want to make in the world.

3. Let go of the things you can't control

Running an online business means understanding the boundaries of your control. Balancing between short-term and long-term goals, you need to let go of things you cannot control and focus only on that which you can control. Letting go is a skill that we need to practice both in personal and professional life, but when we run our business we have to resist the temptation to seize control.

Some of the things we can't control include how soon our followers become clients, how many people "convert" when we run a campaign and whether or not we can consistently bring in revenue. In the beginning there are many things out of our control. We should focus on building the momentum and let go of our desire to manipulate the outcomes because it will bring new scars and result in more frustration.

4. Plan your small steps and make them one at a time, to avoid burnout

Where do you want to be in six months? Most business plans require a five-year vision, but it's hard to predict how online business will change in that long time span, so dreaming in six-month increments is not only less intimidating, but more practical.

Without plans, our dreams are nothing but good ideas that challenge our ability to build something sustainable and satisfying. Many might say, "Yes, I want an online business where I have a passive income stream, a few products that sell, and a community that loves what I do and is loyal to my vision." Then three years down the road they are still where they were because they are waiting for a perfect moment, can't see beyond the day-to-day struggles and feel like they need to know more before they can make any decisive steps.

It's like waiting to lose weight before you work with a fitness coach. The reason we go to the gym and ask a coach for help is so we can learn how to achieve our goals, but many people never make it there because they don't feel like they're "fit enough" to get started.

5. Review

This is a part of cultivating mindfulness, but I would like to emphasize this because when we are building something new we tend to focus on what we *haven't done yet,* which adds to frustration, anxiety and overwork.

Sometimes I have to tell my clients to write down all the things *they have already accomplished* so they can see their progress and enjoy it.

Celebrating milestones, however small, is a liberating experience that will allow you to experience joy and satisfaction on your journey.

6. Forgive

The etymology of the English word *forgive[ii]* suggests its meaning as "give up desire or power to punish someone." We need to let go of the grudges we hold against our former employers or clients. We need to stop punishing ourselves and our business as a reaction to the hurt we experienced in the past. Writing about this in our journals is the first step on this healing journey.

Our traumatic experiences are what brought many of us to this new stage of our lives: opting out of the "real job" and moving into building a job we believe we deserve. Creating an environment that helps us *thrive* in our new job is something *we alone* choose to do. Dealing with our past hurts and choosing to rise above them is where we all must begin.

> *"Of course it hurts, darling. Use it! It's what artists do. Life has wisdom of its own. It dumps shit on you and stirs you up until your soil is fertile. Accept the challenge and plant some seeds. This is how artists grow."*

> — *Kathryn Craft*

CHAPTER 2.
Adopting 5 Important Mindset Shifts

INGA* WAS IN HER MIDDLE THIRTIES, married and had an energetic 2-year-old son. In our Skype lessons where I taught her English, the camera was always off, to save the bandwidth, but I'd looked at her picture on social media, and was surprised how my mental image matched her looks: her dark hair pulled back in a ponytail, small eyes, hasty and unnatural smile, and a pointy nose.

Inga spewed out complaints like some sort of revolting sickness. "Whatever works," I thought. "At least she's practicing her English." Even for the 30 minutes of our lesson, her husband struggled to keep her son occupied.

From time to time, the boy broke into our lesson with loud cries and calls for mama. I imagined her husband in another room, sprawled out on a sofa, watching TV or playing computer games or maybe taking a nap. But hey,

Inga never failed to remind me, what did I know about her life? I was 32 and had no children.

Inga didn't prepare for her classes because she was "always tied up with the child." She winged it for the most part (thinking I wouldn't know) and then indulged in a blame game asking why I hadn't taught her how to memorize the words better. I'd been dealing with such abuse for over six months because I believed that "the client is always right," but now I was beginning to wonder. Inga loved to argue about my prices. She begged for discounts and had no gratitude for the many compromises I'd made for her.

On one particular day, she opened up our session complaining. She told me she'd tried to talk to a native speaker in a social event, but "kept forgetting simple words." Now it was my fault, and I knew nothing about teaching. My methods were wrong, and maybe we had to focus on some other assignments than what I'd prepared for her.

When the lesson was over I was fuming. "How dare she treat me like this? Why am I letting her get away with it?" I asked myself why some lessons were a delight and hers was a torture. I pondered the whole purpose of me teaching online — to have a say over who to teach and why.

I realized that the money she was paying me was not worth the emotional labor of listening to disrespect, complaints and even abuse. I took a deep breath and typed up a quick email,

"Dear Inga,

After our lesson on Wednesday it became clear to me that I will no longer be able to continue our work

together. I think I have helped you to a certain point, and from now on someone else might be willing to continue. I am sorry to inform you like this, but we will not be meeting from now on. I can recommend a few other teachers you might want to check out for your further lessons. ..."

The email was followed by more complaints and arguments, but my decision was firm. For the first time I felt like I had control over situations I used to have no control over when I taught at college, and exercising it empowered and liberated me.

. . .

"Our ability to grow is directly proportional to an ability to entertain the uncomfortable."

— *Twyla Tharp*

Have you ever thought that our lives consist of strings of small events, all interconnected with each other, impacting us in more significant ways than we realize? How often do we hear the advice "not to sweat the small stuff," and in a number of situations this advice is important. It allows us to keep moving forward.

But I'm thinking of the small things that happen every day that we deem insignificant or learn to tolerate because "that's the way things have always been," "it's hard to make money," "I have no other solution," etc. We're afraid to change anything, and because each individual thing is "so small," we just let things slide, for months and years.

Small things, such as doing menial tasks on our own even when we can afford to delegate them, tolerating a bloodsucking client just to pay the bills, giving away discounts and "special offers" without regarding the bottom line of the business, wasting time looking for disparate answers to our many "small" questions.

Such small things make a profound effect on our business, and there will be no sustainable future when they are disregarded or swept under the rug. In this chapter we'll look at some small things that we need to reconsider in order to bring inspiration into our work and to the people who love what we do.

1. Say 'no'

I find that often we can't say "no" because we're not centered in our "yes." Saying "no" gets easier as we become secure in what we do, what we want to be and what change we want to see in the world.

But as teachers we face a difficult task of moving from *helping people* to *helping specific people achieve specific results.* Most of the time we don't know what specific people might need our help or how we can assure the best results. When we're not clear on the specifics, our work becomes bland.

In this case I recommend starting with a personal soul search. Ask yourself what you love to do and what you could do even if nobody paid you for it, what you believe are your "superpowers" and how the right people can benefit from them.

That will help reframe our thinking from "when I say 'no' I lose *this* client and *her money*" to "when I say 'no' I win time to find a *better client* who will pay me *what I am worth* to get the excellent results I can deliver."

"No" is powerful and liberating, if you discover your "yes" first.

policies

2. Make 'less is better' your mantra

I don't know how many times I've tricked myself into believing that the more I work the better results I get. We turn ourselves into martyrs, feeling guilty when we take an afternoon off to read or draw instead of working on our website.

We have to teach ourselves to "stop" before we lose our steam. In the end, "tomorrow is another day" is a perfect phrase to keep telling ourselves when we feel like we "have to" hoard more tasks on our to-do list to make "tomorrow easier."

It's a lie. Hoarding tasks won't make our to-do list shorter, as each day has enough trouble of its own. So let it go. Do as much as you can and as best you can.

3. Take a break

Over the years I've learned that I have to **plan** my breaks. If I want to "unplug," I must block my phone notifications. If I want to be away, I have to book a trip and take care of the logistics. If I want to take a break during the day, I tell myself I will only work for one hour, and then I'll shut down the computer and read or journal or draw.

The "breaks" don't have to be long. Start with 10 to 20 minutes, but plan them. I've read somewhere that calling them "mini-vacations" will give our brains something to look forward to, **which will increase our productivity** and mental health.

Don't feel bad about giving yourself a break. Take the time you need to relax — you'll double your energy when you return.

4. Praise yourself

Have you ever worked with a severely negative employer? The one who forces you to work weekends, doesn't give you vacation or bonuses, tells you you're worthless, pays peanuts and always criticizes your effort? I think that when we "hire ourselves" we become the worst version of such an employer.

The negative talk doesn't stop, and it makes us feel less confident in what we can achieve. I've found that praising ourselves and counting all the good things we've done during the day is a challenging but empowering task.

It doesn't come naturally to us, because our desire for progress tricks us into thinking we're lagging behind. But negativity doesn't inspire people to do their art — praise does.

I won't go into the "dangers of praise" as is sometimes debated by teachers, because I believe that, when self-directed, there's never too much praise. Incorporating just a little bit into our daily lives is a struggle as is. So make an effort to think of yourself as a winner, and you will feel like one.

5. Connect with others

It's easy to get wrapped up in *our business,* our problems, our struggle to survive and our projects. Connecting with others or helping others along the way seems like an impossible task. "I barely have time to *do this for me.* When do you expect me to go on forums or participate in discussions?"

One of the paradoxes of life is *when we open up our hands to help others,* we receive incredible blessings. I've found this to be true in life, work and business. It's easy to clench our fists, holding on to the little "progress" we feel we own. We become paranoid that to help others we'll have to let go and lose everything we've gathered.

But when we make **connecting with others** a priority, we'll learn that our success is intertwined. Don't downplay what you can give. Don't tell yourself that you will only engage "when you have time," or "when you're smart enough," or "when you have wise words to contribute." Even if all you can do is lend a listening ear or tell others that you don't have it all together either, you'll both gain a new perspective and will be more inspired to continue.

Our growth starts in our minds. No matter how many hacks we learn or tools we purchase, changes in our work start with changes in the way we think. When we find clarity and say "no," when we prioritize rest, when we praise ourselves and connect with others to learn and grow, our business will thrive. Despite a number of appealing ads that promote easy online business "blueprints," building something worthwhile boils down to how much we value ourselves, our time and how much we respect others. Mindset changes are not "small or insignificant matters," they are a foundation of our healthy future.

CHAPTER 3.
Embracing the Long Journey

IT WAS ONE OF THOSE ROUGH mornings when the heaviness of uncertainty, anxiety, fear and doubt felt like a weight pressing on my chest, clouding my thoughts, suffocating me. I was finishing off my breakfast when the tears started rolling one after another, dripping on the cloth placemat, triggering a few deep-seated sobs, forcing them to come out.

"I can't do it anymore," I said to my husband, who by then had heard this sentence enough to stop what he was doing and listen. We'd moved to New Orleans just a few months before, and I'd decided it would be a good time to stop teaching on Skype and reshape my business so I no longer felt enslaved by running to teach one more lesson.

That morning I felt like the newness of life, the foretaste of adventure, the excitement of the move and the vision of unlimited business possibilities had worn off. I found myself in the grind with waning hope and focus.

Although it had been a few months, I began letting my insecurities shoot up like unruly weeds in an abandoned garden.

"I can't do it anymore. All these months of social media engagement, list building and online marketing, and I still haven't gained one new client. I'm going to start teaching German on Italki." My tears were dripping faster. I put my head down on the table and let those few sobs out.

"I have no idea if this will work out. I feel like I can't break through, and I always think to myself, what if people see that this experiment was a flop? What if I will never sell products or courses? What if people don't trust me? I need to be realistic and stop this nonsense. I need to go back to Skype lessons. I hate them, but at least I know that they will always work. I'll just teach German for a change."

I caught my breath after this emotional outburst. My husband was quiet. The kids were playing in another room, giving us a gift of a heart-to-heart conversation that couldn't happen whenever we wanted, not after kids entered our world with their rambunctious personalities.

Wimbai was sitting back in his chair, thinking over what he heard, sinking deeper into his counselor role, ready to ask me a question. I didn't know what he'd ask, and I dreaded it. A part of me wanted affirmation, but he'd never run a business, he had no idea what I was going through. A part of me wanted a quick resolution, a helpful shortcut that would end the discomfort.

Finally he asked, "Do you think you're expecting results too soon?"

He didn't just ask me this, did he? I'd written about it in my blog posts, discussed it on social media, preached it in my webinars. I realized I was fighting against my self-imposed timelines and greed for quick and easy outcomes. Another prominent coach's success story blurred my vision, and instead of writing my own story, I focused on replicating someone else's. That brought nothing but disappointment and apathy.

. . .

"Show up. Consistently. Keep creating content. Speak passionately to a crowd of 0."

— Regina Anaejionu

We've all been there: looked at someone else's snapshot of success, posted across social media, ripped it off and pasted it into our brain. Later we called it "our blueprint" and worked hard to replicate it, only to experience disappointment in the end.

A few years ago I crossed paths with an online teacher who wrote consistently, showed up every day, created valuable lessons for language learners and shared them generously. I was intrigued and amazed to find such incredible dedication, such commitment and a sense of purpose.

Yet, six months later, he launched an online course and then disappeared. After a few months he inboxed me asking for work. It turned out that his online course didn't sell, so he had to regroup. The regrouping has taken at least a year, and I haven't heard from him since.

Gone.

The online world is a gigantic incubator of ideas. Many of them hatch and die, undeveloped. The ones that survive aren't necessarily the "fittest," but most often the "grittiest." Those that hang on a little longer than others communicate that they are serious about their work, **are the true believers** and are **committed** to making their ideas work.

Confidence and commitment communicate the value of a brand. Even in the fast-paced and transient online world, commitment, passion and grit evoke trust. Our potential clients don't give away trust the way people pass out free flyers at the mall. Trust is a treasure that they share only with those who they believe deserve it. Which means, as online teachers and recipients of such trust, we will not receive it after a couple of weeks of intensive work.

There will be a long and excruciating period of time when all we'll experience is silence. Eager to get some traction in response to our consistent work, we'll try to force it, look for a shortcut, a magic solution, a quick fix, but waiting is our only choice.

So, are we willing to commit to the 'slow fix'?

Here are **four qualities we need to cultivate** to accept the longer route, stop looking for a shortcut and prevail in the face of difficult circumstances.

1. Patience

Patience is the ability to bear or endure. Enduring doesn't happen when things go according to our plan. Enduring takes place under pressure. When I was hungry for results just months after I'd switched to working smarter, I realized (with the help of my husband) that I was being impatient. Based on my research and experience, we need to multiply our most optimistic timeframe by three. So if we hope to have a fully booked schedule within one year, we should expect this in three years, if we do things right.

While we wait, we need to identify what's beyond our control and focus only on what we can change. For instance, we cannot control how many people buy our product, but we **can control** the creation process, the marketing, the testing, the tweaking, the copywriting, the spreading of the news, etc.

Often teachers obsess over the wrong things, which adds to the stress. I've learned in my years of entrepreneurship to ask myself, is there something *I* can do about this situation? Once I find the answer, I will focus on what I can do so I worry less.

2. Curiosity

Instead of asking *why,* ask yourself *why not.* The life of an entrepreneur is about discovering and testing out new things, and you cannot do this without sincere curiosity. "I wonder what would happen if ..." should become your work motto.

- What would happen if I tried this approach?
- What would happen if I offered this?
- What would happen if I tweaked this?
- What would happen if I connected with this person?

I am sometimes surprised at how comfortable we become with the linear thinking that the traditional classroom instills in us. We believe that **this is the only way** and refuse to challenge our own beliefs. We turn into the dreaded version of the stuffy academic environment we ran away from, and eventually develop habits that are hard to uproot.

One of the most common questions I hear from clients is, *"Can I really do this?"* When I suggest they should connect with a group of people, run an event or write a book, for instance, I not only hear this question but a series of reasons **why this idea won't work.**

I'm amazed at how eloquent and logical we become when we explain why something we haven't tried before won't work. This is nonsense. Be curious. Ask yourself, "What if?" You have no idea where your curiosity may take you. If nothing else, it will take your mind off of incessant and useless anxiety.

3. Courage

Courage is our ability to follow our curiosity in the face of fear and potential failure. It requires faith and determination, grit and perseverance, but most of all **courage compels us to** *act* **on what we believe.**

If we believe that people's lives would be more meaningful when they learned a foreign language or a new skill such as writing, we should **talk about it,** inspire people to take that step toward their dreams instead of hoping that somehow they will "get" this point on their own.

When we second-guess our every step at the beginning of the journey there's no way we can convince our audience to believe in us, to believe that our cause is worthy, that we're doing it because we care. So often I talk to people who start out with a lot of determination, only to see the resolve wane in a few months.

Setbacks are always lurking in the background, but it's impossible to move forward while doubting. Find a support group, work with a coach, read books and stay the course. Remember that the first year is the hardest one, and keep pushing through.

If you are not courageous enough to step into the unknown, how can you expect your clients to do the same while working with you?

4. Generosity

Always look back and think of how far you've come. It may seem insignificant because we often experience the tension between where we are and where we want to be, but take a moment to look back at your journey and **help someone along the way.**

Generosity is the greatest remedy against a funk because it helps you shift your focus from "how hard it is for me" to "how much I can do for others." Whether it's a small donation, a shoutout on social media or just a listening ear, there's a lot you can do that will help others. In turn, it will help you, and that's why you **should** do it.

Seth Godin wrote that "generosity generates income," and I've come to believe it's true. When I invest in the work of others, I somehow get business coming my way, or if nothing comes immediately I remain more calm and content in the face of more challenging circumstances.

When I give, whether by donating toward a fellow entrepreneur's project, buying their books/products or letting the world know how incredible their work is, I become alive myself. I stop seeing my problems through a magnifying glass, but rather — through a microscope. I gain a new and valuable perspective on running a business — that one day people will remember me not by how much I made but by how much I was able to give away, to share, to help others.

The ultimate reason for all of us to build a business is so we can build wealth (whether financial or creative) to share with others, but we shouldn't wait to start sharing *when* we achieve a "certain level." We can begin now, making small steps and gradually increasing our giving so we're not only consumers but conscientious collaborators.

I must say that nobody likes waiting. If any of us could take a magic pill, find a shortcut that will save us from the excruciating vacuum of uncertainty, we would certainly make it easier on ourselves. But gaining traction in your business takes a lot of time, and the sooner we break with the urge to find a quicker and easier solution, the sooner we'll embrace our reality.

Our reality is that we'll wait longer than we expect, and our results will not show for some time. While we're waiting we can either quit or continue with patience, curiosity, courage and generosity — in the words of Lesya Ukrainka, we should continue sowing the flowers amidst the frost.

CHAPTER 4.
Staying Ahead of the Market as an Online Teacher

"CREATIVITY IS MY PROBLEM. I keep creating products and then kill myself marketing them. I've created a maze of sales funnels and automated sequences, and now need to hire someone to help me manage this overwhelm. I can't keep myself from creating, but do you think there is a way to do it without losing my mind in marketing and sales?"

I was talking to Veronika Palovska, my new graphics designer, brand strategist, coach and web whiz extraordinaire. Just a couple of years before, she had signed up for my new accent training course and left a remarkable review. I stalked her online profile and checked out all the courses she was taking at the time. In the wide online world that was the closest version of a first introduction.

A few months after that, her name would appear among my active subscribers, then social media followers and later — customers. She bought everything I'd put out, so hiring her opened the door into the insights I could never have generated on my own. Hiring a fan would pay off in invaluable currency coming from someone who cared.

"I think having a lot of products is a good problem to have," Veronika reassured me. Her words glowed with encouragement and positivity, something my inner critic never possessed. "We should create a library."

"Oh, no. A membership site?"

My fears began speed-painting the gloomy picture of why the idea was impossible. Recurring payments, never-ending marketing, tech issues and maintenance expenses. Building engagement in a forum with online teachers who were not sure about technology and engaging with others. Who would want to pay me for that?

Veronika kept talking about how a library is such a great concept, how we could encourage connections and inspire people who want to take action by giving them an affordable opportunity to create their future together.

I still wasn't sure but found myself discussing the logistics of turning strangers into a tribe, to inspire engagement with each other and to keep them coming back. My inner critic would remind me of the two prominent coaches who'd closed their membership sites with grave disappointment, but I thought to myself that I could at least try.

Eighteen months into the "experiment," after monthly tweaking, measuring and "smartifying," I found myself watching with surprise as my recurring revenue kept climbing, despite my predicted gloominess. It seemed like a miracle to me. Although it wasn't one of those "overnight" miracles as some might imagine. It took eighteen months to accomplish what I had originally thought would only take only six.

. . .

"[If] you work on the awareness of the space you inhabit, especially the negative space, you will easily be able to imagine what's not yet there, what there is for you to bring."

— *Philippe Petit*

The online world is changing fast, its trends mixing, mingling, fading, dying out, emerging out of nowhere. Being aware of the trends will keep us alert and agile, but we must never lose connection with *our* reality, values, convictions, talents and vision of how our work can transform the world around us.

Pursuing the latest fads will disconnect us from our calling and the people we would like to serve. Instead of seeing their specific learning needs and providing efficient solutions, we will constantly be obsessed with how much money we can make by becoming a bestseller on Amazon, launching a signature course or building a membership site.

Our marketing has to center around a specific client, not faceless "blueprints." So what if it didn't work for others?

Who cares if it's something that "gurus" disregard based on their "vast experience"? We choose the medium that will help our clients engage and grow together. We don't push them to try out something that we feel "will work because it's what's worked for others."

But how do we stay ahead of the market? How can we discern what is the best choice for *our community* at *this moment?*

Here are some simple strategies I recommend:

1. Connect with your audience

When I ask online teachers about their business strategy, eight out of ten will use the same phrase, "I'd like to create and sell an online course." People have used it so often that it's now a cliché.

Why not investigate first if your audience *needs* an online course? Perhaps you should get to know this group better? You can run free or paid events, do office hours, invite people to sign up for short sessions with you, raffle products and packages, and connect via chat. When you start out by "creating an online course," you forget who it is for and perhaps even miss the fact that your audience may not need it at all.

2. Engage outside your niche

One thing that has helped me recognize trends and come up with new ideas is engaging with people **outside my niche**. Hang out with writers, readers, illustrators, web designers — and see how you can apply their wisdom to your business.

Because I'm a part of several communities online, I'm amazed at their creative ideas, strategies and implementation. They may have nothing to do with my niche, but one unusual idea sparks another one, and in the end I come up with something original. On the other hand, when you focus only on consuming content inside your niche, you risk sounding like someone else.

3. Flex your creative muscles

If you let it, creativity will help you connect the dots that other people will never notice. Those who don't prioritize creativity usually have "no time" to draw or doodle, write, do crafts, arrange flowers and just create something new.

Taking time daily, or a few times a week, to do things that inspire us and awaken our creative genius is a must for a thriving online teaching business. One of the reasons I find platforms that promote 1-on-1 language teaching confining is they do not give you any creative freedom to explore other ways to teach online. As a result, teachers sell out their time and then find no way out of a system that imprisons their creative spirit. Take time to explore your creativity. Get into the habit of surprising yourself.

4. Work smarter. Work less.

I believe every online teacher should strive toward working less. But working less isn't about doing nothing; lazing around on the beach while your magic online course pumps passive income into your account. Working smarter is a mindset shift that needs to happen before we can create passive income streams.

We need to question our obsession with overwork and overwhelm. We need to challenge our notion of productivity and efficiency. We need to define our productivity not by the number of tasks accomplished per hour, but by the number of unimportant things that we choose to let go.

Working smarter starts with spending less time on our day-to-day duties so we can design our lives and find fulfillment not just in work, but in other things that inspire us and make up our lives: food, travels, reading, language learning, family, friends, pets, music, theater and others.

The core of working smarter involves decentralizing our work and bringing the things that matter to us back to the center.

5. Read

Reading is distilled creativity and pure pleasure. I challenge myself to read something different each month: new authors, short fiction, forgotten classics, contemporary bloggers, emails, children's books, magazine articles, headlines, email subject lines, ads. When reading a particular contemporary piece gets tiring, I dive into classics because working through complex language while you read adds an extra delicious layer. Try reading in foreign languages, even if it's for a short time.

I used to think that unless I had several hours a day to spend with my favorite book, reading wasn't worth it. Now I've changed my perspective and take a book even to the gym. Instead of scrolling through my social media feed, I read a couple of paragraphs between exercises.

Nurturing my soul brings forth an unexpected harvest of ideas and concepts. But more than anything, reading makes me open to change.

Change can be scary, especially for the teachers who love order, lesson plans and predictable routines. Yet, when we run an online teaching business, we need to learn to embrace change, dance with it and empower others to do the same. Only when we see ourselves as change-makers, and not mere transmitters of knowledge, will we be able to build a sustainable online business that impacts and transforms. Reading will help us achieve that.

6. Hire a coach (an extra bonus if he/she is a fan)

Because my self-criticism loves shouting into my ears and crippling my confidence, I've come to believe that hiring a coach is essential to keep moving forward. Whether you do it in a group setting or 1-on-1, for an extended period of time or to help with a project, you need to find someone who will spark your confidence and cheer you on as you learn to step over your own doubts and fears.

In my case, hiring Veronika to coach me through the tough process of product creation management has given me insights into the minds of my customers and allowed me to find a medium that would work best for *my audience*. For me, working with coaches has meant moving faster and becoming more confident, which, in the end, has translated into more business and connections. It's not the product or service that sells, it's our confidence. For instance, creating a new online course will not guarantee sales unless we have the confidence that speaks to our audience with authority and explains clearly why the course is relevant.

I know how tempting it might be to look at your lack of time and money and decide that coaching is outside of your budget, but try to be creative about it: join coaching programs, groups, challenges, work with a community of people that will spur you on. When you get outside of yourself and let someone else give you encouragement, you will accomplish important things and find the confidence to navigate through the unknown in the future.

Staying ahead of the market doesn't mean you need to turn into a magician who divines the future and learns what stock to buy. If you don't want to be lost in the fast-paced online teaching world, make it a priority to connect with your audience. Change the way you work so you can make time for the people you work with, people you can learn from, creative tasks to help your original art blossom, and books to challenge and change your mindset.

CHAPTER 5.
Experimenting With Online Teaching Formats

At some point I became a crutch to one of my students.

Dennis* had worked with me off and on for a year hoping to improve his speaking score for a test. I couldn't get him to practice outside our meetings because he had come to believe that by showing up he was improving. I knew that I couldn't keep creating new assignments and charging him for that because he needed to move past 6.5 and get an 8. But because of our frequent meetings, he wasn't motivated to do more work outside of class. As a result the low score persisted.

Until I told him there would be no Skype lessons anymore.

"What do you mean? That's the way we've always worked."

"Dennis, the way we've always worked is clearly not working. For you to get a higher score you need to do more homework. To motivate you I will reduce the number of sessions to one a month and give you voice-chat assignments instead."

"So I'll be recording myself?"

"Every day, as many times as you wish. And if after one month you see no progress, we'll go back to 1-on-1."

"OK."

The first time I doubted the efficiency of Skype lessons was when my client believed that just attending sessions with me meant getting closer to his goals. Sometimes it worked, but in this case it didn't.

A month later we had a short consultation, and Dennis said he couldn't believe all the progress. His next statement surprised me: "I think we should continue working like this."

Three months later he took his test and got an 8 in speaking. We'd done a year of Skype lessons before with no significant results.

. . .

"I have not failed. I've just found ten thousand ways that won't work."

— Thomas Edison

Turning from a coach into a client's crutch is painful. It's hard to acknowledge because you keep telling yourself you can shake things up a little by introducing a new activity, or choosing a new textbook or even creating extra workbooks for this client. It takes guts to take **yourself** out of the picture and recognize that it's in the client's best interests to have less time with you.

In Chapter 4, I shared the lessons I've learned about being curious and agile if you want to continue to stay ahead of the online teaching market. But how do you do that? What does it mean to change the familiar format of online teaching? In this chapter we will take a look at the process of shifting formats, from conventional to original.

When we doubt *ourselves as professionals* or *are unwilling to question something we've always believed as true,* we build walls that separate us from unlimited possibilities of running an online teaching business. Instead of experiencing and *practicing the freedom* that online work brings, we stuff it back into what we know. Let's see how we can rethink the familiar and try out something new.

Step 1: Acknowledge that people can learn in different ways

At some stages in their lives, people might enjoy learning in a group setting. At other times, 1-on-1 in real time is a better option. But are these the only opportunities that allow us to grow? Don't we also learn when we read a book, take an asynchronous program, attend an event, or even follow someone on social media?

Think about your ideal client and where she is in life. Is she a single mother, or a busy CEO who will not have a minute to herself? Could you inspire her to learn through something different and unconventional?

Step 2: Don't impress the masses, work for the audience of one

Fed by advertising, we've come to believe that online teaching is about "the masses." More students means more money, and for many it becomes a final goal.

Most teachers believe that they need to offer *a lot* to attract *the masses.* What they don't realize is such "diversification" increases their workload *exponentially,* so in the end they make even less. If you teach people from different backgrounds and different levels, you'll have to create more materials and provide more support than if you focus on just one group.

Creating your brand with just one person in mind is like creating white space in your interior design. White space accentuates **the central piece of furniture in the room** and pulls all other pieces together in harmony. However, when you have **too many furniture pieces** and less white space, your room will turn into a cluttered storage space that confuses your visitors.

The more you learn about your ideal clients, the more attractive and creative your offer is going to be for them. Not taking that time to get to know your ideal clients will cost you time and money and will bring you a lot of wrong people that will either want a cheap, quick fix or a free ride. This is when they no longer value your exceptional services and see you as a crutch.

Step 3: Acknowledge that choosing 'one' excludes everyone else

I still struggle with this point. My natural inclination is to help everyone. Every time I sense a person isn't the right fit for me, I get frustrated with myself and want to push through anyway. **Somehow I feel like I'm not "professional enough" if I can't help everyone.**

But let's look at doctors, for instance. When we have a specific issue we will prefer to see *a specialist,* not a general physician. Assuming that all diseases can be cured just by one doctor is ridiculous!

Why then as teachers do we take upon ourselves this unbearable burden of "saving everyone"? Take some time to reflect on **who your ideal client is and why you love working with them.** Then you will be able to attract the right people through your content by speaking *to that specific person.*

Step 4: Push yourself to go beyond the familiar. Brainstorm

When I help clients create products and services, one of the sentiments I often hear is, "I can't come up with anything more creative." What that means is they've only listed a couple of options. The concept of *brainstorming* 20 to 30 ideas before making a choice sounds tedious, yet it's **the most effective strategy to get your creativity flowing.** So challenge yourself to push beyond the top two options through brainstorming.

To brainstorm, take a blank piece of paper (not ruled) and think about your ideal client. What is her life like? How can she fit learning into her busy schedule? What types of activities will reinforce her to give it a try? How can you facilitate the learning process?

If she wants to learn to write, is there an app that she can use to put down a few sentences in writing every day? Is she more creative and would like drawing or doodling as a part of her learning process? Is she the artsy type who would like to create her own artistic journal? Is she a literature buff who loves writing out quotes and talking about them?

Step 5: Offer a new format as a temporary solution with the client's best interest at heart

Let's say several of your clients see you as a "crutch." They've stopped growing and are now relying on magic by spending an hour a week with you. You want them to challenge themselves, do their homework, be inquisitive and go beyond what's in front of them, but they're rolling deeper into mediocrity.

This is the perfect time to try out one of the formats you've just brainstormed, with fewer 1-on-1 sessions and more versatile self-guided assignments. **When you offer this to your client, expect resistance.** Don't present it as "permanent," tell them you're going to "try it out" for a short period of time.

If the format works, the client will ask you to continue in the same way (or will be less reluctant to go for another month). If the client cannot find motivation and continues with unhealthy scepticism, then *you* need to decide whether this client is a *good fit for your business.*

Experimenting with formats can be scary, but this fear is driven by our natural resistance to anything unfamiliar. When we find the courage to explore the unfamiliar and welcome it as a part of our business adventure, we will give ourselves permission to be different and feel confident about it.

Sometimes teachers are compelled to start their online business journey by asking the wrong questions: "Will

this format work? Will people **get it?**" By asking these questions they use fear to crop out endless possibilities, and that cripples their business.

Don't let fear tell you what format won't work. Go back to your ideal client and see what will suit her best. Also choose the format that fits with *your lifestyle, nourishes your creativity and gives you more freedom.* If one format drains your passion and robs you of joy, maybe you should change the way you teach. You **have a say** in how you inspire others to learn, and it's okay to give yourself permission and freedom to reinvent the learning environment once again. So go and create: a workshop, a workbook, an email course, a writing studio, a community of like-minded people who want to learn from you and with you.

CHAPTER 6.
Creating a Product to Discover More Freedom

"Do people just want free stuff from me?"

I'd been writing a new post weekly for about a year, adding "buy a session with me" as my main call to action. Even though my blog was becoming popular and readers were leaving comments, responding to my emails and even booking free sessions, I couldn't sell my coaching packages.

At the time I was charging $90 an hour, and getting new clients felt as painful as pulling teeth. I wondered if it was my price (too high or too low), my blogging style (too much information for free) or my audience (not ready to buy). Most online gurus would find fault with the audience, calling it "incapable of investment." I refused to believe it; after all, the iPhone was a hefty investment, yet the price didn't deter people from buying it.

Digging for answers on my own brought about more confusion and overwhelm. How could I inspire people to invest in coaching without sleazy schemes and salesy barking? By giving away too much, wasn't I teaching people to enjoy my free expertise forever? Would I ever be capable of selling anything?

In retrospect, I don't think I recognized my client's journey at the time. It hadn't occurred to me that asking for a sale at the end of a free blog post was like asking a first-grader to solve an advanced math problem. No amount of inspiration will work in this case, because the first-grader hasn't mastered simple addition yet.

Regardless of our learning styles, in order to master anything we need to learn to use what we already know if we hope to solve something more complex. Learning is about forging paths from the known into the unknown.

The sales process works the same way, though at the time I didn't know how to connect my "simple math" with my "advanced math" offer. I had a vacuum between them, so despite the popularity of my blog, a small but active list of subscribers and a steady stream of free session bookings, the coaching continued to be a hard sell.

There had to be something in the middle to set the sales machine into motion. I decided it had to be an e-book. Following the advice of Breanne Dyck[iii], I participated in a small product challenge and published my first book, "Opted Out of the Traditional Classroom" — a selection of recycled and edited blog posts from my first year of blogging.

Thirty people I didn't know purchased that e-book and went on to buy more books, programs, events and even coaching in the future. The small e-book filled the void between my offerings, moved my cautious audience to action and forged the path in to the "advanced math." These first readers became my most loyal clients and brand evangelists.

. . .

"Your book is your business card."

— *Michelle Prince*

Many online teachers I coach struggle with the problem of not being able to sell their services. If you've ever asked these questions, then you've wrestled with this problem as well:

- Do people really care about my work?
- Do they only want my free stuff?
- Why do they never buy from me?
- Am I putting out too many free materials?
- Am I attracting only freebie hunters?
- Is my audience not able to pay this much?

From my experience, not being able to sell more expensive services stems from the void between the free and paid offers. Here's how it evolves. First, you struggle to find clients for your 1-on-1 classes. So you lower the price, sell out your time, get exhausted and frustrated by the cheap clients.

To solve this problem, you raise your prices, lose your clients and begin creating content to attract a different type of client. You attract followers and fans, but they are hesitant to join your coaching programs.[v] Now the gap between your free content and your paid services is even bigger than before: you've got a void on your hands.

Some people aren't comfortable working 1-on-1. They may not have the time, the resources or the schedule to allow such intensive training. Others think they aren't "sure yet" if they can justify the investment. Then there are those who will say that one hour can't be effective enough. And there will be those who will tell you they're getting "a lot more value from your free stuff already," what's more to learn? **Graduating from a blog reader into a coaching client is a heavy commitment.**

So by offering free content leading into a higher-priced product/service **you've created the void** that keeps people from paying you money.[vi] In this chapter I'll focus on how to fill that void, how to create your first product on which you can later build your entire brand. I'll walk you through three main milestones that will lead you in the direction of making more higher-price sales.

Milestone 1: Choose your small product

It doesn't have to be an "e-book"; it can be any digital product that doesn't require you to be present for the sale to happen. Think about a workbook, a book of quotes, a planner, an inspirational guide, etc.

One thing to keep in mind is your product must not only solve a particular problem but also tell your story and infect your audience with your vision. So it's important to share your *why* with the audience, not just the *what* and the *how.*

Your product **must be useful but not overwhelming.** Overdoing on volume is the same as not giving enough. When people are drowning in layers of content, they won't be motivated enough to practice the strategies you shared with them. Focus on one problem and offer actionable solutions.

Milestone 2: Recycle what you have

Those blog posts or podcast transcripts you've already created can be great material for your book. Most teachers already have enough materials to offer to their audience; they just need to put them together, structure and edit them.

If you've made a product already, you can relaunch it by changing part of its content and improving its design. When Veronika Palovska and I decided to write a book together, we took what we had already (my first book), made the title more compact, used the outline and rewrote each chapter. Then she redesigned the cover and we began selling the book on Amazon. This is how "Opted Out of the *Real Job*" was born.

We could have written something new, but we already had a vibrant community that aligned with our vision and values, so why not relaunch the same book?

Milestone 3: Build your community around your small product

Your small product can become the foundation of your brand. Writing "Opted Out of the Traditional Classroom" prompted me to start my Opted Out community on Facebook. With Veronika's help we later created the Opted Out Planner, relaunched the book and designed a journal — all with similar branding.

A year later we launched the Opted Out mastermind — an intensive training program for online teachers and coaches who want to build their own teaching businesses online, the smart way. With each new "product" we spent less time marketing, because we already had the community and the vibe with which people resonated.

Instead of creating an array of new products, think of creating **a line of similar products** and services. If you wrote a fiction book, why not create an experience around it: a weekend retreat reading the book, a book club, a lab for people who want to read and write fiction, a workbook with learning prompts based on the book, etc? These products will stack like matryoshka dolls and make product creation and marketing easier.

Making your first product is liberating and addictive for the creative souls of teachers. Once you sell your first book, the temptation is to "maybe write something new." But it's smarter to go deeper into that one product by offering more services surrounding it. It's also smart to keep building momentum even after the launch, so more people learn about your work, join your community and choose to work with you. Writing and publishing a book has never been easier, but one book isn't an end in itself. You have a lot more to say and share than one book can possibly hold. Use it as a foundation to create services and other products that will help your clients be more thorough when achieving their goals.

CHAPTER 7.
Growing Your Tribe the Unconventional Way

"WHAT WOULD YOU SAY is your niche? Who do you help? How do you do that and why?"

I'm in a coaching session with a new client* who has maxed out her time teaching English to students from all walks of life, charging low fees because "in this country nobody will pay me more, and this is the going rate." She wants to work smarter but is uncomfortable with the harder questions. My "digging deeper" exercise doesn't make sense to her.

All she wants is a series of tips so she can passively sell her new online course to an impressive crowd of 30,000-plus followers. She's surprised that instead of telling her what exact words to put in a sales email and how often (and at what times) to send it so she can sell her course, I veer our discussion into the area of niche.

I feel torn because, on the one hand, I want to help her solve her problem, but I realize that the problem she thinks she has is different from what it really is. She believes that by adding tricks and crafting special automated sequences, she'll be able to sell more of her products. After all, she has more than 30,000 followers. I believe that these numbers are elusive and vain, that in order to sell she has to build a solid and focused brand that attracts loyal customers, not those who prey on free or cheap stuff.

So I go with my gut and focus on what she really needs, but my direction doesn't convince her.

Her email comes a day later,

"I'm sorry to say that our session didn't help at all. What I wanted is for you to teach me how to convert my current followers through automated email sequences. I wanted a structure, a system that would help me sell passively while I teach select students 1:1. Instead, you took me on a long detour of niche finding. I don't know why it was necessary since I've been working in this niche for so many years, and introducing something new will mean losing my followers and current students. I already have a brand, all I wanted is your help with email marketing. ..."

My heart sinks, and as always I begin asking myself what went wrong and why I wasn't capable of helping her. I click "respond" quickly, but stare at the pulsing cursor, wondering why it is so hard to communicate that a large following doesn't equal automated sales, that tricks don't build a tribe and that running an online business is a step of courage that sometimes means re-evaluating our work and starting from scratch. I wonder why, indeed, it's impossible to turn thousands of followers into thousands of dollars — how easy it would have been if it was all about the right tricks.

Yet sales are a byproduct of bringing something meaningful to a select group of people who share the vision behind your work. This is when your work turns into art, and you become indispensable. This is when your "following" graduates from discount hunters to proud shareholders. This is when your brand's absence translates into a loss.

. . .

"Each man's life touches so many other lives. When he isn't around he leaves an awful hole."

— Clarence the angel in "It's a Wonderful Life," a 1946 Hollywood classic

When we think about growing the tribe for our online business, we focus on a group of people who become our fans and brand evangelists, who are willing to share our work and invite others to do the same. This is the most common approach to tribal dynamics: We need a tribe of like-minded people who will buy our product and tell their friends about their incredible experience.

In this chapter I want to look at this subject from a different angle. I want to talk about *our responsibility* to build a vibrant community of people who grow in order to help others grow. Whether it's three or 30,000 people, we as its leaders determine the tribe's health and prosperity. I believe a prosperous tribe is one that **benefits every member, not just the leadership.** Our challenge is to shift the community from being *leader-focused* to *member-focused.*

In a healthy tribe both leaders and members care for each other's well-being. Making money is a byproduct of a healthy community, but it's not the end. A community is there to help everyone grow.

It's a place where **everyone learns to give,** not just to take. The leader then is responsible for **creating and cultivating such a vibrant and nurturing ethos.** It's a place people **want to join,** where their contribution isn't measured by the amount of money they pay for products, where the goal of **helping each other grow** becomes central.

When we build a community like this anything will be possible. **But how do we do it?** How can we work with our random readers, busy subscribers, distracted followers and turn them into **engaged shareholders of our brand?** How can each one of them become a cheerleader without being prompted with a carrot or, worse yet, a stick?

Here I'm going to share five quotes that have shaped my understanding of a thriving online community and helped me build one — not focusing so much on the numbers, but rather on the nature of the group that shares my vision.

'A rising tide lifts all boats.'
— John F. Kennedy

I used to worry about giving away too much. It was hard to draw the line between giving certain things for free and offering paid services. "What if I *overgive?*" Ironically, this anxiety didn't stem from my **cautious generosity,** but rather from a **concealed greed.** The moment we ask ourselves "how much is *too much*" and worry about giving away *anything* is the moment when money becomes more important than relationship-building.

While I believe that moneymaking is a lifeblood of any business, we cannot start our tribe with the money and **insert money** into every conversation. That's why keeping a job (or finding a part-time gig) is a smart way of building your business as it allows to avoid money stress and resentment toward people who request information but aren't ready to buy yet.

Once I realized that setting artificial limits on generosity was tough, I decided to give away as much as I could. Whenever my work slowed down, I used that as an opportunity to give away my time and expertise for free. But that's not the end of it.

I also used my authority to promote the work of others — the projects that I found inspiring and unique. I didn't do it with any secret agenda, nor did I charge people for a *casual mention* of their name in my blog post. I did it the same way **I would hear others talk about the people that inspired them.** Sharing a story and praising the effort.

My words helped these people get noticed and connected. They also inspired them to **keep going,** and as their business was picking up, so was mine.

When I saw Veronika Palovska's site[vii] I fell in love with her branding. I knew that one day I would hire her. I had no idea how I would do that or where I would find the money, but when later I ran a successful program and made a couple of thousand dollars in one launch I knew where to invest my money.

My first project with Veronika drew people's attention to her brand. I was endorsing her work, and soon she had clients of her own that contracted her for their design projects.

In the mindset of "concealed greed," some people hesitate to promote others thinking that somehow it will thwart their own success. But quite the opposite was true for me, and it will be so for you if you choose to **lift others up** and support their work through small tokens of recognition.

When we lead our tribe, we need to get to know the people, see their potential and inspire them to grow beyond it. You will not need to force people to buy from you if you show genuine concern. Taking care of others has never been a poor strategy.

'When the reader hears strong echoes of his or
her own life and beliefs, he or she is apt
to become more invested in the story.'
— Stephen King

"How can I get my product to sell?" a teacher would ask me. "Do you have any tricks?"

The best trick I know is to **learn to listen to our audiences.** Often we resist hearing feedback because it makes us feel uncomfortable and unpolished and forces us to change. Nothing has been so awakening as hearing a client tell me that I put out too much content. No matter how much I love writing, I discovered that less volume (or short and more digestible content) is more valuable to my audience.

Spending more time listening and forcing myself to write less with more impact helped me to find new clients with less effort and improve my copy as well. If we are more aware of our clients' needs when we write our copy, it speaks to their hearts, making the sales process more organic.

I've heard teachers talking about "enticing" someone with their sales copy, but in my experience that alienates your ideal client. We only "entice" when we try to convert the wrong person. Any time we invest ourselves in the wrong crowd we'll get poor results, no referrals and endless pricing discussions. What we should do instead is **listen to the right people,** swallow our pride and do what they say.

Listening is the core of a healthy tribe. Pay attention to the comments, likes, surveys and discussions. What are people saying? What are they *trying to say?* Knowing what people want **before they realize it** will help you to create products and experiences that will be appreciated and therefore sold. Selling is a complex process that isn't only about putting out a product and using gimmicks to force people to buy it.

'To take off you must place yourself against the wind.'
— Philippe Petit

Taking off is a labor-intensive process. Think of being on a plane: the noise level, the shaking and the rattling, the persistent fight to gain momentum, the charging forward despite the forces that pull you back.

Indeed there is more resistance as your business takes off, and as you begin to *climb* to the right altitude you need to stay the course and keep moving forward. There are a lot of unknowns when you build your tribe. The numbers are few, the discussions are not happening as often as you'd like, sometimes you lose the sense of direction and wonder if any of this work matters.

Always keep in mind that **a takeoff doesn't happen unless it's against the wind.** A community doesn't evolve overnight, and the beginning stages are the most challenging.

Keep going. Find a support group, coaching programs and masterminds that will help you gain momentum even as you're moving against the wind. When you learn to overcome, you will know how to encourage your own tribe when they find themselves "against the wind," ready to take off yet wondering why they "can't cruise yet." There's a lot of work that needs to take place before things "get easier."

'... if you only do what you can do, you never have to worry that someone else is doing it. It keeps you from competing. It keeps you looking inside for what's true rather than outside for what's popular.'
— Delia Ephron

Comparison is a game where you'll always lose. You'll lose because there'll always be someone with better credentials, a prettier website, more memorable content, impressive copy and greater money. Looking outside will make us feel like we will never measure up, never achieve anything, and will always remain where we are.

Some time ago, I unfollowed several people whose work made me play the comparison game. I'm not immune to it, so I thought I would just stop following their work. After I unfollowed their posts, ads and blog updates I realized I had more time to think about **my own tribe,** their struggles and how **I could offer my help to them.**

Because I focused only on what *I* could give, I came up with more original and unusual solutions than what was common inside my niche. That attracted more people and got more people talking about what I was offering. People would join my community by word of mouth, having heard about my programs from people in **other online groups.**

The more original you are, the more attractive your brand becomes, the more unique your tribe. If you spend your time comparing yourself with others, the only thing you'll perfect is trying to **outdo someone else.** Competition doesn't bring originality, it only strives to borrow from others. Soon your brand will be a copycat version of someone you want to be, and there is nothing worse in online marketing than faking someone else's story. Not only does it not work, it doesn't attract loyal customers because people can smell fake from afar.

Authentic tribes grow around originality and creativity, so look inside more than outside.

'People with passion look for ways to make things happen.'
— Seth Godin

When you're passionate about your work, you **will build a tribe of equally passionate people.** Passion is contagious;

that's why I always ask my clients if the thing they want to pursue is what they are passionate about. Often people are inclined to do something online just because it worked for others or perhaps it's something that "will definitely pay the bills." But creating a tribe based on "what's *in*" or on our "qualifications" (if we're not passionate about them) will result in empty numbers and loud noise; it won't inspire people to **change.**

When people see that you are passionate about your work, they will be sold on your vision as well. No amount of "gimmicks" will sell the stuff you're indifferent about. In the end, it leaves a bitter taste in everyone's mouth.

So ask yourself what you're passionate about and don't forget to communicate it to your tribe. Sometimes we lose ourselves in strategies, steps, tips and tactics (I do it all the time); that's why it's great to have your core message spelled out in front of you — the core message you're passionate about, that will propel you and your tribe to move forward.

When you lead, lead with passion.

As a community builder you don't lead numbers — you lead people. To be more effective in this work, think of inspiring and promoting others' work and accomplishments, listening to their experiences, sticking with them through thick and thin, offering creative and original solutions and sharing your passion. I want to emphasize that community building is not a one-day endeavor, but it's a long-term process.

Keep in mind that your community won't develop by itself. As a leader **you** decide what people discuss, post, promote and say to each other. You, as a leader, have the permission to set up rules and follow through with them. If you hesitate or feel insecure about your leadership role, your tribe will turn into something you won't recognize, a Mowgli raised by the wild beasts of the internet. Any tribe needs a leader, and you should be one for yours. Don't let others determine your direction. Stay firm and focused.

CHAPTER 8.
Writing That Transforms and Affects Change

"HI. I LOVE YOUR POST!

I am an underpaid, very good online English teacher working for a company as well as a live Math tutor in my city. I'm hoping to offer English classes by myself online next year.

But I've really experienced what you said here. I tried doing group classes at an affordable rate, thinking that students will come by the hundreds. But they barely came, cancelled 20 mins. before the time and shunted me around.

While my 1on1 clients, who pay me quite well for here in South Africa, come on time and only cancel when something REALLY demands a cancellation. And they don't have a problem paying what I ask! Literally, no one complained all year. They realize the value of their children's education and tutors as professionals.

Now I'm wondering whether I should increase my hourly rate. There is a good chance that I'll increase it by 6.6%. And I like what you said about professional development. I take that very seriously."

I was staring at my screen in disbelief. How could it be? I'd started this blog just a month before, and putting my uncouth writing into the black vastness behind my screen felt awkward and scary. I'd kept another blog four years prior, updating it several times a week with the most helpful language learning tidbits my qualified linguistic self could muster, yet received just a handful of random comments over the years.

But now, a few weeks into writing on a subject where I had the least "professional expertise," I was engaging in life-changing discussions. Was I dreaming? How come nobody was asking me for my MBA diplomas with honors before commenting? Why was my price-setting post connecting with the audience more than my tips on how to use media in the classroom?

Unpolished and clumsy, my words and sentences spoke my heart's message with courage and resilience. I discovered that when left passionless, expertise turns into a haggard old lady, wagging her finger in reproach, never reaching her hand to connect. My first blog could have won all the stars and banners from the experts, but it didn't bring me closer to my audience because I'd only used it to showcase my expertise and stayed silent about my passion.

. . .

"Writing is telepathy."

— *Stephen King*

Another blog post hits the online space, and we don't know what the future holds for it. We wonder how much value, insider tips and brilliant professional advice we should share before we are heard. But what if it's not about our expertise *first?* What if the goal of our writing online is not to clone encyclopedias and textbooks?

From my years of writing online I believe that our words and sentences make the most impact when we connect with the reader, when our hearts and minds interact with each other the way we'd chat over coffee. Instead, a number of online teachers (my old self included) tend to turn their online space into another conference podium where the speaker sprinkles her expertise across the room hoping to impress and reaffirm herself.

Stephen King wrote that "description begins in the writer's imagination but should finish in the reader's." I think to deliver a powerful written message, whether on the blog, in a social media post, or in a 150-word bio, we need to train ourselves to read our audience's thoughts, down to motives, utterances and specific words.

How do we become mind readers? I've got five surprising strategies designed to help you see the world from your reader's eyes so you can connect with your audience. These are the unconventional writing tips to tackle linear thinking and monotonous copycatting that make your writing bland.

1. Find your audience online

You can't take shortcuts here and you must resist linear thinking. If you teach English, avoid claiming "English students" groups and forums as *your audience.* Unless you want to spend years stamping out freebies and yelling for some vague English learners to pay attention to you, **think through who you want to work with.**

You need to join groups and follow people who share your *why.* If you want to work with busy professionals teaching them to slow down, appreciate their progress *and use language* as a medium, then hunt for groups where these productivity freaks hang out.

If you want to inspire people to travel to Spain and *learn the language as they prepare for their trip,* don't look for language learners, look for travelers.

Your audience doesn't need you to spoon-feed them exciting "grammar" points or other expert tips. You need to make them hungry by pointing out **the reason** they need to learn this language or by connecting each tip to something incredible and desirable on the other end.

2. Eavesdrop

What does your audience say? Don't write until you listen to their voices. Join online groups and forums, search platforms to gain insights into the questions that spark your audience's curiosity. You strike gold every time you find a question, a comment or a phrase that you can later expand on in a blog post, a video or a podcast.

Whenever someone *in your audience* mentions a book or a podcast or a movie, check those out. Read the reviews, look through the backlinks and all the extras. This sounds like taking an online course on your audience, but it's what we need to do instead of *thinking that we know it already* and making decisions based on *our perception of the audience,* not on the real people.

3. Take notes and reflect

This is where I take a piece of paper or my journal and begin writing. Making lists or doodling through the process helps you distill all you've learned and build on it. You can "create" your first products in your journals. You may never sell those, but projecting them is like creating a template for the future.

In one of the discussions I had online, a teacher said she didn't want to charge a lot because she didn't want to be greedy. I thought about this concept and came up with a blog post later that was called "How to Charge What You're Worth and Not Feel Greedy or Guilty." When you take the time to listen to your audience, and connect with them in their own words, they will know you really understood what they were thinking about. That generates trust and turns readers into fans.

4. Engage in discussions

When online teachers complain about "strict rules" in groups that prevent them from "selling," I am reminded that we need to break our desire to pick the most obvious strategy and claim it as the only one. Sales don't start at the point of you offering a service or a product at a certain price. If they do, they usually end there (and then they end your career online).

Many people have made these mistakes, and you can avoid the trouble of building up your reputation after losing it to spamming by sticking to the two simple rules of "online sales:" ask questions and be helpful. Remember that whenever people post a question, there are dozens — if not hundreds — of those who are reading the entire discussion as if it was their own.

So answering to one person sometimes means answering to 50 or 100. The more helpful and giving you are, the more trust you'll gain. Keep in mind that with the way people read and reread comments and discussions, this trust grows exponentially.

On average it takes about one year for someone who joins my free group to buy my product and service. That, of course, is the average number; it fluctuates between six months and two years. Sometimes people connect with me and tell me that the first time they found out about me was when they were reading my answers in some group threads.

So think of your engagement as a seed. This is how your business becomes sustainable. This is how you know you will have clients two years from now — by showing up and being helpful.

Answering in discussion threads also charges your writing batteries. It's like working on prompts — short exercises that polish your overall writing skills.

5. Invest in learning to write

It's surprising to see what some online language teachers call investments: a headset, an extension cord for several screens, a yoga mat, a gym ball, a desk or a computer. While we certainly "invest" in many things that make our work more effective, *investment* in its pure form is the money we put in something that *appreciates over time.* While most objects we need for business are necessary, they are eventually going to fall apart.

Writing is one skill you should consider honing early on because, apart from blogging (which may not be everyone's content strategy), we write on sales pages, in our newsletters, project proposals, product descriptions, and on social media. Academic writing that many of us have polished over the years doesn't help sell products.

So consider taking short challenges and growing in the following areas:

- Generic writing (to find your voice online)
- Copywriting (to write your web and sales copy)
- Creative writing (to rid your writing of clichés and other carefully learned "set expressions" and boost your creativity)
- Tight writing and editing (to cut out unnecessary things)
- Blogging (to create written content that translates into followers and clients)
- Journaling or freewriting (to generate ideas when the blank sheet of paper scares you)

Dig deeper into each of these, and you'll find that writing is a lifelong adventure, and the more it captivates you, the more it will captivate your readers, inspire your audience and infect them with your vision.

The greatest challenge with any writing comes when you decide to send it out into the world: Hit "publish" on your raw thoughts, and send them off for others to judge. This is where self-criticism becomes a recurring pain and perfectionism prevents us from sharing our work with the world.

I think perfectionism fades when we choose to see our work through the lens of documenting the process of growth. Just as taking kids' pictures and adding them to the album creates a treasure book of memories, showcasing our work at different and often rough stages documents our journey into mature writing. It allows us one day to look back, see our growth, and find the tiny seeds and sparkles even in our first and clumsy writing attempts.

CHAPTER 9.
Overcoming Perfectionism

MY SECOND BOOK LAUNCH wasn't as stressful as the first one. I had written that book for my audience only, scheduled all the launch activities, paid for formatting and now could enjoy my 35th birthday, having a slow family dinner at home, with a few sales clicking in the background.

In the book I shared my journey toward working smarter. At the beginning of that year, I had challenged myself to make money without 1-on-1 clients. It had been a scary decision, but I knew that without it I wouldn't discover more freedom and satisfaction from my work. In the book I had shared my numbers as well: the hours I'd worked from the time I began teaching online full time, the money I'd made, and how that ratio had changed over the years, leading up to my decision to work smarter.

The process of writing revealed a lot of my own insecurities, fears and vulnerabilities. I was going beyond words and sentences, I was sharing my story, my "success" metrics; all of those numbers felt so personal, and I wondered what the reaction might be.

A few days after the book launch, I began receiving feedback. A teacher who had been following me for two years shared his disappointment. "So after doing all this work online for two years you only made $2,000 a month?"

That was the reaction I'd been anticipating when I chose to make all of my personal records public. A simple question that in my mind grew to the monstrous size of mockery. "Who are you to share your story and call it successful? Why should I even listen to you?"

The reader's reaction revealed his definition of success — the amount of money made — while I wanted my audience to see the time-to-money ratio. If two years prior I was making the same money teaching 25 students a week, this time I only had one client and several group programs that were generating the same amount. Going from 30 to four hours of teaching a week and being paid the same didn't strike the person as a change. If the numbers were the same, what was the big deal?

All of a sudden I felt compelled to "undo" my book. To unpublish every word until I reached the "success" my reader envisioned for me. Mine wasn't a "perfect" story, and maybe I'd shared it too soon. Should I have waited until I could fly my own jet? The thought of "disappointing" someone in my audience felt like an unforgivable faux pas. "I've been found out, and I can't continue like this."

. . .

> *"... better an imperfect dome in Florence*
> *than cathedrals in the clouds."*

— *Twyla Tharp*

In my experience, perfectionism comes in a multitude of forms and shapes. I may not have suffered much from the "impeccable work" syndrome and always preferred "done" to "perfect," but I've been tempted to polish up *my story,* so it sounds more accomplished and successful. I wondered if my rough edges and failures would discourage people instead of uplifting them.

Yet the main reason for *me* to start my blog was to bring a less polished story into the world. That's what I needed before I started — to know that small and simple ideas, less glamorous investments and modest hours can still lead to a thriving business, even among the chic and exclusive, six-figure coaches who have it all together.

In my journey I've discovered that nobody has it all together, and our work online never ends. A brand is like a growing tree, and at different stages of its development you experience new challenges and bring in new ideas to define your work and streamline your process.

When you look at your business from this perspective, it's easier to let go of the gripping desire to cross all t's at every stage. We do the best we can, and tomorrow we will do better.

So how do you deal with perfectionism? Shall we just ignore it and force people to push through? If there's one thing I've learned in the years of building my business it's this: "Just do it" is not only lame, but also ineffective. Sometimes "just do it" is the wrong strategy, because it can destroy your brand before you have a chance to develop it.

This is how online teachers spend months creating online courses for an abstract audience (just so they can "do it") and then hiring a coach to help them with marketing and sales. Or they start building their website (or even invest in branding) with a vague idea of what their business will accomplish.

Here I'm summarizing four strategies that have helped me and my clients move the needle. I know from experience that you can put these ideas to use, even when your business is small and scrappy.

1. Know your strengths and weaknesses

Sometimes our weaknesses conflict with our desires to make things look and work the way we want. Talented online teachers spend hours formatting documents, setting up social media, doing dull paperwork instead of outsourcing this work to those who can do it better.

In the end they fail to make something look perfect because they don't have the skillset or the expertise. They doubt themselves, get frustrated and mad for no reason.

A simple solution is to hire someone to help you out. If you feel overwhelmed at the thought of how much *outsourcing all these projects might cost,* think of one small task that can make an impact on your business. Do you spend a lot of time creating images for your social media? Why not hire a graphic designer who would create a series of templates and guidelines for you so you could spend 10 minutes instead of one hour?

The time that you save can be used to invest into your *strengths.* That way you will gain more confidence in what you do and will accomplish your tasks without delays.

2. Be simple and don't compare

Comparison turns you into a slave. It's impossible to move forward when you spend your days looking over your shoulder, trying to be like someone you admire. Her website might look cleaner, her blog neater, her images more professional and her Twitter feed more focused.

I've learned along the way that **when I can't be like someone else, I should strive to do things more simply.** I used to spend hours fooling around with my sales pages when I should have been engaging with my potential clients. I wanted to make my website look like another freelancer's (who happened to be a web designer, too), and I kept feeling frustrated when my work didn't bring me the results I wanted.

At some point I made a decision to make the labor-intensive projects simpler and my work — smarter. I would spend more time talking to the audience and connecting with my potential clients, rather than adding layers to my sales pages. Later I was able to hire a web designer to take over those projects, and I haven't looked back since.

3. Set up deadlines

> *"A schedule reminds me: time is of the essence, in life as well as in a project ... Whenever I plant in my creative path a time-bomb, a reminder, a deadline, it frees me from Time. By reminding me that I can distort Time. The deadline feeds my impatience. And often because of that I find myself ahead."*

> — *Philippe Petit*

When you can't finish a project on time because you keep embellishing it, there might be different reasons for it. Some people make tweaks because they are not sure if this is the project they *should* be working on. They doubt their work before it's complete. You can resolve that by hiring a coach and working on your strategy *before* engaging in a never-ending project.

Other times you struggle to get things done because of this desire to make all things perfect. The more you work on this, the hungrier your perfectionism gets, the more demanding. This is where you have to establish deadlines and stick to them.

I understand that some might see deadlines as too "studentlike," "intimidating" or "limiting." But if you reframe your mindset about deadlines, you'll discover that **they are healthy boundaries that inspire you to keep going.**

Imagine if you ran a marathon *without distance markers or milestones.* At first you might enjoy the run, but soon you'll be wondering about your progress. Create such milestones for your work by setting deadlines or time-markers. The work you'll accomplish at the end of each milestone will be your reward.

4. Show up every day and do the best you can

People have said it so many times that it has become a cliché. I'd like to look at this old cliché from a different angle. When I look back at the last two years as a business owner, I find that I've had only a couple of "big highlights," like being featured on a large Facebook page, selling out a program in a few days, launching a new book and selling it to people I barely knew.

Those highlights are incredible, they make you feel like your efforts are paying off, but after a few days of sunlight, there are more bland working days when people don't open your emails, don't respond to your requests, don't find you relevant, "share-worthy" or even successful.

It's on those days that I have to give myself an extra-motivational pep talk, ask myself why I'm doing it, and show up. I need to go back to my business buddies, draw strength from them and keep going. The showing up is harder than the "highlights," because **for every highlight day there are months of seemingly invisible work.** Months of no emails, fewer client inquiries, lower sales and tough decisions. But without showing up there will be fewer things to celebrate and more overwhelm to deal with.

I suggest finding a community of people, not a Facebook crowd, but a community of engaged people who will help you show up no matter what. Prioritize the overall big projects you want to do, and you'll discover you'll have more inspiration to complete all of them on time, even on dreary and bland days when you don't feel like doing anything.

> *"Perfectionism stops people from completing their work, yes — but even worse, it often stops people from beginning their work."*

> — *Elizabeth Gilbert*

My desire to perfect my story kept me from speaking it with courage and power for over a year even as I was blogging and building my audience. I felt like I wasn't *enough,* that I had to be like someone else to *deserve* the attention of my audience and that I had to seek approval with my every project.

Then I began reflecting on my own strengths and how my *messy story* encouraged others. Perhaps the one disappointed reader was not my ideal client after all. Perhaps his thoughts of success were not supposed to define mine. Perhaps he was fighting his own demons of inadequacy and imperfection. Who knows? I'm thankful to him for revealing to me that instead of hustling for someone's approval and perfecting my story, I should approve of myself, my current effort and my unique journey.

You are the person who determines your own success. *You* are the one who chooses whether to be overshadowed by your imperfections or to *use them* to make your story authentic and convincing. I believe you don't need to have it all together to empower people to change. You've worked hard today, and today you bring your best. The sooner you stop making your work worthy of someone else's unrealistic expectations (or even your own ideal standards), the more growth will take place.

CHAPTER 10.
Dealing With Money Fears

"So HOW MUCH DID YOU CHARGE him for your lessons?"
I asked Marina* while sipping on wine in the surgery-white
kitchen of a dated but orderly two-bedroom apartment that
she rented. A festive plate in front of us sported sliced
cheese, olives and pastrami.

"$30 an hour. That's my usual rate, and like I said,
he is a bigwig in the City Council, so he can afford it. ... And
what do you charge?" she asked closing her eyes and tilting
the wine glass to her lips.

Marina* was an English teacher like myself. We'd
met each other at a conference years before and became
friends. She lived in another city, and once every few months
one of us would make the trip to see the other so we could
catch up on work, books, language learning and life. At the
time I was still juggling a couple of classroom jobs, along with
an overbooked tutoring business. Marina's work challenges
were similar, and we found a lot of encouragement

from each other. We talked business, clients and numbers. Then in the evenings we'd hit theaters or raid bookstores.

But one thing unsettled me. I couldn't believe the brewing envy and aggravating sense of unfairness that were nagging me even though I wanted to enjoy our time together. Marina was charging her clients double what I was making per hour. The comparison would knock me off my balance and challenge my self-worth. "What's wrong with me? Am I not as qualified as Marina? Why can I not charge as much?"

Then came a flood of thoughts dancing in my mind, convincing me I couldn't charge more. "She lives in a bigger city. She pays more for her rent. She spends more money commuting. I'm fine where I am." But was I? If I could work less and make more, I'd do it in a heartbeat. Why wouldn't I? Was it just the money or my own warped sense of worth?

I discovered as I was wrestling with these thoughts that my fear of not having enough, and losing what I had, kept me from dreaming bigger and accepting that I wanted something different for myself. Somehow I shamed myself for wanting to use money to access more opportunities, more freedom, more travels. Somehow every time my money fears came up, I sensed that it was bad and dirty and unbecoming. In the end, they were ruining my own peace of mind and a great friendship.

. . .

> *"Fears prevent us from trying new things,*
> *including experiences that can fulfill and*
> *fortify us. We miss out on the necessary*
> *experiences that can shape us into the*
> *people we most want to be."*

> — *Meera Lee Patel*

When I set out to write a chapter about fears, it was hard to imagine where the journey would take me, not because I don't have fears, but because there are too many of them. Covering them all seemed overwhelming.

As I reflected on the most common fears I've discussed with clients and have seen recur in my own life, I knew that I had to deal with the scariest of all — the money fears. I think we need to face them before we build a business that brings in money for us to support the life we want. After all, if we are afraid of the thing we'll talk and think about on a daily basis, it will be challenging to experience it.

This chapter isn't about affirmations or the law of attraction. I would like us to take a look at our money fears and see beyond them: where they come from, what they indicate and how they prevent us from pursuing our future.

Sometimes I like to compare fear to pain. In the physical world, pain prevents us from getting hurt. We touch a hot object and jerk our hand away — if that didn't happen, we would lose skin. Pain indicates that something isn't working properly and needs attention. In a way, pain is the physical mechanism to keep us safe and healthy.

Fear works the same way in the realm of emotions. It indicates risk, discomfort, impending change and wants to prevent us from going down that path. Sometimes fears are legitimate and helpful. But when we run an online business, fears can either fuel our journey and help us achieve the impossible, or keep us anchored where we are.

When it comes to money and business, fears get complicated. On the one hand, running a business that generates a fair income helps us envision a life that we would like to achieve. On the other hand, this idea is jolting to anyone who has experienced some share of money stress and learned to live with little means. Somehow our past struggles with money make us feel unworthy.

Language teachers often juggle multiple jobs and side-gigs. Many run toward having a business so they can find relief from the constant pressure of being busy with no money. Yet, from the moment we have to decide how much to charge, how often to pitch, what to sell, how to market and what to give away, we go back to the charges that a school offered to *us* and attempt to run a business on it.

In a way, we go back to the bind we ran away from, except now **we are that boss that doesn't pay.** Even though we have control over how much we charge, we feel ashamed of thinking about it, unworthy of asking for money and greedy for charging above the "going rate." Just like in my story with Marina, I had a choice of raising my fee, but I felt paralyzed by fear and by all of the scenarios of what might happen if I lose all of my clients.

While fears are complex, there are specific tools you need to use to overcome them. Just like in language learning, the more you use them, the better you get.

Here are several steps to help you deal with your money fears every time they arise.

Step 1: Acknowledge your fear

An online teacher once wrote to me, "I don't think I have any money fears, but I don't think the people I'm working with will ever pay me this much." This statement has an internal contradiction. If you are worried about what people can or cannot afford, you **do** have money fears.

I believe the only people in our industry that don't have money fears (and therefore build successful businesses quickly) are those that don't come from the teaching background. Say, for instance, a business executive got tired of working 80 hours a week and decided to run an online business. Generally, because of a different relationship with money, this person might be able to risk more, charge more and not feel guilty about it.

Otherwise we all have money fears. Let's acknowledge them and write them down.

Step 2: Get to know your fears

Where do they come from? What story are they telling you? What are they "protecting you" from? At some point I always ask my clients to write their money story (stories). Most of them come back listing all their shameful, negative associations, fears and anxieties. A few were too ashamed to even write them down.

So write your money story, paying attention to the language you use, your family dynamics, your work history, your own perception of what you can achieve and how. Also ask yourself *why* you are afraid of making money decisions. How are these fears keeping you from taking action, growing your business and staying consistent with your progress?

Step 3: Think beyond fears

Write or draw how different your life would be if your business could fulfill your needs consistently. You might call it daydreaming or children's doodling, but this powerful exercise opens your mind to the possibility of charging more, building a sustainable business and selling products and services on a regular basis. Fears don't allow you to travel that road, and once you listen to them, you will never see a different reality.

Imagining yourself in a world where you can make what you deserve without feeling guilty or pressured or greedy doesn't mean the physical change will come overnight. But it will make you more courageous to step into the uncomfortable business world with more decisiveness.

Coping with money anxiety

I would like to tell you that once you've "gone through the steps," your fears disappear. I wish I knew how to do it myself. But the steps are there to help you go through money-related worries multiple times, until they stop taking hold of your future. They will never go away completely, but you will be able to discard them sooner and change your behavior.

When I get overwhelmed with money fears and anxieties, I ask myself several important questions:

- How did I deal with this last time?
- How were my needs met?
- Am I worrying about something that's immediate or something that might happen in the future?
- What can *I* do right now to change the situation?
- What do I need to let go?
- What should I do *instead of* worrying about things I can't control?

Money fears take time to explore and reroute, and running a business will bring them up to the surface. Avoiding them will keep you in a rut for too long.

However uncomfortable they make us feel, facing our fears sets our business in motion. Many online teachers I've worked with have taken up meditation, calligraphy, doodling, journaling, writing, yoga and other mindfulness activities to help navigate through the fearful unknown when the situations they are facing are out of their control.

The result has been a positive personal transformation, a more philosophical and even transcendent perspective on situations and a number of creative solutions that people who are stuck in their fear trenches can't see.

Perhaps that is the one big benefit of dealing with fears: becoming the people we've always wanted to be by transcending the scary situation and looking at it in a more mature way.

CHAPTER 11.
Working With a Coach as a Way to Build Resilience for a Long Journey

"THE LAST COUPLE OF MONTHS have been really hard. I've had to work on my mindset, deal with anxiety and money issues. On the positive side, I took some time off and went snorkeling and enjoyed my day on the beach."

I began coaching Elfin Waters in 2016 when she realized she wanted to go beyond Skype lessons and build her own business around her passion for the Italian language and Italy. By then, teaching on a third-party platform had worn her out.

The depressing feeling of exchanging hours for little money and working with people who didn't value her work pushed her toward a new solution — building her own business that would impact and empower people with the tools they need to immerse themselves in Italian without spending hours working on it.

Elfin had started teaching online after a serious accident that left her with traumatic brain injury. What used to take minutes was now taking hours, and her previous workplace didn't suit her anymore. Teaching online was an escape, an opportunity to feel useful and to contribute to someone else's growth.

In over two years of working together, Elfin gained clarity on her message, began speaking it with confidence, started growing the tribe around her "All About Italian" Instagram account, spoke at events and guest-posted for a number of popular blogs. She also created and sold her first program, launched her biweekly newsletter, designed her first workbook and began planning a unique Italian immersion experience.

While some things may have taken less time to accomplish, others were draining: building a website, writing copy, doing research on her new project, not selling some things (as we had hoped), having fewer clients; but the hardest of them all was surviving anxiety that came with the seasonal loss of clients.

I always looked forward to our sessions, because I admired her resilience and willingness to keep going even when it was tough — and her sweet smile and insightful language that spoke to my heart and inspired me as I was going through a low business season, too.

"So what helped you deal with your anxiety and money stress?" I asked, taking note of Elfin's persistence and her extraordinary ability to mine the dry and dreary rocky surface for tiny diamonds of positivity.

"I did a lot of writing and meditating," she replied. "Every morning I would write down all the heaviness on my heart. Just offload it on the paper. The meditation has been helpful, too. And learning to breathe. Being aware of my breath to reduce anxiety and stress. Throughout my dry season this daily practice was what carried me through — that and going back to why I started this business altogether."

Write. Breathe. Meditate. Go back to the Why.

. . .

*"Mentoring is rarely about the facts
of the deal (the facts are easily found),
but instead is a transfer of emotion
and confidence."*

— *Seth Godin*

When language teachers look into joining my coaching programs, their immediate goals are specific: tools, hacks, strategies, tech tricks, etc. The expectation is often that a coach is like a magician, the owner of trade secrets that unlock unlimited business.

What they find while working with a coach (especially in the beginning) might be disappointing. In the beginning, their coaching benefits have little to do with the hacks and more with the mindset. They learn resilience, patience, stress management, fear management, collaboration in the community, confidence and commitment.

Professional soccer coaches call this process *conditioning* and never start practices without it. It's not just about the mastery of the game or the technique. It's strength- and resilience-building that allows soccer players to run for longer periods of time, avoid injuries and carry the heavy emotional burden of competitive sports. One thing that strikes me when I follow the World Cup is that there are more losses than wins. Only one club wins big; everyone else is behind. Obviously, players need to be *conditioned* to go through these intense experiences.

I believe that coaching is central to our success as online business owners; it helps you save time and reduces your stress levels. But I don't mean that all this will happen overnight. Still, especially in the beginning, it's easy to chase after the wrong things and lose your core and clarity.

There are usually several objections to coaching that I've come across, and I would like to dive into each of them. I want to make you aware of different formats and choices for coaching and prevent you from spending your time looking for quick fixes that don't work for everyone. In the end I'll share a simple strategy that will help you choose the right coach for you.

1. I don't need a coach, I can learn things from books (or Google)

Imagine you take a free course, read a number of books and attend a dozen webinars on how to teach online. If you're not overwhelmed at that point, you will implement everything and wait for the result. Sometimes it might disappoint you. What's next? Where do you go from there? How do you know your next steps? How can you be *sure* that what you are doing is going to work *the second time?* What if it doesn't?

More information is not the answer to our business questions. Information overwhelms and paralyzes action-taking. You need the assurance, confidence and support, you need to *hear it* from someone who has walked this road before. In that sense, books and other resources are limited.

2. I get so much coaching for free (via blogs or webinars), why hire anyone?

Free coaching scratches the surface. It is a highlight, a movie preview, an attractive ad. It gives you the taste, and (if done right) will give you enough courage to make that first step. And even though a journey starts with the first step, **one step is *not* the whole journey.**

Working with someone on your specific situation will empower you to keep going. As you show up for your sessions or (if you're a part of a paid community) participate in the life of the community, you will see milestone after milestone on your new journey.

3. I should only work with a coach that provides me with certificates

I believe that it's our *client,* not a *certificate,* that makes us business owners. We own a business when we have a person who pays us or a product that sells, not the certificate that hangs on the wall or the article of incorporation or a letter from the mayor congratulating us on registering our business.

What does the certificate of *Excellence as an Online Teacher* offer us? In the years of running a business **nobody asked me if I had a special certificate.** People chose to work with me because they had read my blog or watched my videos. Some had read my "about" page and felt like it resonated with where they were on the journey.

If you're looking for a certificate, please know that it's not **the highest trust-building asset.**

4. I don't think I can work with the same coach for a long time

You don't need to work with a coach for a long time. Depending on your goals, you can work on a project and then take a break, then go back to it. I've worked with different coaches on different things: strategy, copywriting, email marketing, sales, time management and creative writing.

With some of them, it was several sessions, with others – just one. Sometimes I joined coaching programs where several people are working on the same problem. You may choose to work with someone longer, but if you have smaller projects/questions, it's fine to work for a shorter period of time.

5. I don't have the time/money

Coaching comes in different formats. Some are more costly because they offer more support and 1-on-1 work, others are less expensive because they are based on the assumption that you get as much as you put in.

Membership communities are an example. For an affordable fee you can go every day, ask questions, work on assignments, collaborate and create events together. In the end, you can get quite a bit from a paid community, *if you are willing to change the way you work.*

Whenever I've hired coaches to help work on projects or get clarity about what I'm doing or how to do something better, I've tried to refer to specific "hiring guidelines" that have helped me make the right choice. There were times when I hired a wrong person, and that experience itself confirmed that I should have looked over my "guidelines" first.

The guidelines are now my compass when I need help and am looking to hire someone. Feel free to use or adjust some of them for yourself:

1. Don't rush to hire a coach
2. Take your time to get to know the person through social media, a blog or a newsletter.
3. Join a free session (if available) to see how you may work together.
4. Don't allow anyone to push you into something you're not sure about.
5. Choose someone whose work philosophy you want to emulate.
6. If given a choice, go with the coach who is familiar with your line of work.
7. Be ready to take advice with a grain of salt.
8. Always ask if the coach offers continuous support.
9. A coach that helps you improve and grow as a person is an excellent choice.
10. Beware of coaches that guilt you into buying from them.

When I began giving Skype lessons in 2010, I knew nothing about coaching and the possibilities it could give me as a business owner. Then I discovered how long it took me to **decide** what to do next and to **know for sure** that this is the most efficient strategy for *my* business. Sometimes the research took me down long and windy rabbit holes, so instead of doing the work and making a difference, I was spending all of my time *figuring out* and making sure that my decision was going to *pay off.*

We've all been down our rabbit holes, and I say it might be time we left that futile pursuit. If working 1-on-1 sounds intimidating, start out with a coaching program or even a community where you can be learning, growing, making connections and developing your brand surrounded by like-minded people.

Finally, set the right expectations. At the very beginning you're learning the ropes: building your resilience and stamina to get ready for the marathon. Making money is the finish line, and there is a lot of running to be done to cross it. A coach will help you to get to that finish line, to see that you build a sustainable business and that you are able to choose wisely for the future. But you can't cross the finish line after you've barely started. Get ready for the long journey, and make sure you're not doing it alone.

CHAPTER 12.
Leading, Not Just Teaching, Your Community

"So you're saying I should tell my audience what they can and cannot post? Can I really do that?"

Fiona Young, a hardworking, driven and ambitious English language coach, had contacted me to help her build her test-prep business at AngloFlow. She had started at zero, and four months into the process her new group had grown to more than 1,000 members. She had made changes to her website, built relationships with specific people in the group and was finishing off her workbook to help students with the writing part of their test.

As with any community, the goal was to provide help, build trust and establish authority. In the group, students would post their written assignments and ask Fiona for feedback. With dozens of people joining every day, however, the forum was becoming so noisy and busy that

Fiona found herself flooded with requests, questions and comments.

Her own messages to the group with the updates of her upcoming book launch would be swallowed by the rapid feed, drowning among endless requests for feedback. Most frustrating, of course, was that the numbers of active forum participants weren't translating into sales.

As there were no posting rules in place, people spent most of the time sharing their assignments and waiting for feedback.

"There's too much noise in the group, so people just don't notice your announcement. As an admin," I suggested, "you need to decide when people can and cannot post, what they can share, how they should engage and what the purpose of this all is."

Fiona didn't seem convinced she had the authority to make such a decision.

"You are **the leader** in this group, and you set the rules. If you don't do this, nobody else will. The community culture doesn't come out of a vacuum. You can create it by planning ahead what you think will benefit every member and what will motivate them to work with you."

. . .

*"If you want to build a ship, don't drum
up people to collect wood, and don't
assign them tasks and work, but rather
teach them to long for the endless
immensity of the sea."*

— *Antoine De Saint-Exupéry*

How do we teach our audience to "long for the endless immensity of the sea?"

As teachers and coaches we have mastered the art of sharing the information we know and providing feedback. We've turned ourselves into walking encyclopedias who feel the need to provide answers to questions, correct mistakes and reiterate textbook rules. In initial coaching sessions, I often ask teachers what they do well, and 8 out of 10 will say, "I can explain things in a plain language" or "I am patient with my students' mistakes."

Look at a typical online language teacher's social media account, and you will find a multitude of tips, phrasal verbs, gender declension examples and (of course!) conditional sentences. No wonder we cannot turn bland language learning groups (aka freebie hunters) into a vibrant and loyal fan club!

There are entire business brands that focus on grammar-mistake correction only. For some reason, we've turned ourselves into *transmitters of information,* not *leaders of a community.*

Our educational paradigm has shifted away from the knowledge-based approach. When almost *anything* can be Googled or "apped," what is our role as *online teachers?* Should we use our platforms to retell grammar books (in a "fun, entertaining way") or should we dig deeper into the core of our work?

I used to think that *leadership talks* were reserved for CEOs or school principals, businessmen and government officials. Perhaps because of the impact of Russian — my mother tongue — I've come to associate *a leader* (a masculine noun in Russian) with charismatic *men.* Whatever the origin of my "leadership-talk-aversion" disease might be, I'm happy to say I've had to rethink it in the last several years, particularly in the context of leading my own community.

I believe that our roles as *online* teachers, coaches *and* business owners go beyond offloading information in an "easy and entertaining way." **We must learn to lead.** But in order to lead a group of people, we need to learn how to lead ourselves, create a specific vision of *our future,* forge a path to achieve our vision and invite others to follow us on that journey.

In this chapter I'll talk about each stage in more detail.

1. Lead ourselves first

When it pertains to our industry, I'd say that leading ourselves means doing exactly what we would like our followers to do. What needs to change *in us first* before we speak about it to others?

For instance, many online teachers complain about their lack of time, but don't do much about it. Ironically, they get frustrated when *their clients* complain about *their* lack of time. Before we go out trying to "fix" our audience's time problem, we should start with our own. What can we change? How can we be more efficient with less? How can *we* learn to prioritize?

If we want people to leave comments on our blog, we should comment on others' posts first. If we want people to promote our services or products, we should take the time to promote or even buy theirs. If we want people to speak well of us, we need to watch what we say of others on social media, what reviews we leave, how we respond to people with different opinions.

We cannot succeed with *our communities* when we don't contribute to others to help them grow.

2. Create a vision of the future

The first thing about creating a vision is learning to listen. Listening to our audience and hearing their frustrations. Then thinking about our own frustrations and wondering how we can connect the two. In a way, creating a vision is about building a future where **you as an online teacher** can help your client live without a particular frustration.

Here's an example of what not to do. Remember how often you hear the sentiment about dated and rigid textbooks? Well, sometimes the very people who are frustrated about the textbooks are the ones who bring them back in the form of ... YouTube videos! I think changing the mode doesn't change the essence of the problem. By explaining the rules in videos instead of textbooks, we've just *added* to the issue, not resolved it.

So think about something that frustrates you and your audience. Think of how *you* can solve this frustration and then create a picture of the future *without* this frustration. This is your vision. This is what you share on social media. This is, in the words of Antoine De Saint-Exupéry, the "endless immensity of the sea."

3. Show how to achieve the vision

When our focus changes from "transmitting information" to "leading a community," what we share on the blog, on social media and in newsletters changes, too. It's hard to inspire people to "fall in love with authentic Spanish language" if we keep rolling out verb tenses. No amount of "easy rules" will make me *fall in love* with a language.

A changed vision prompts us to *change the path* to achieving that vision. In a way, it's easier to show your "expertise" and focus on sharing rules and grammar concepts. Those are prescriptive and rigid. But they won't build the desire for people to *change their thinking* and enroll on the journey with you.

So how do you forge this new path for your community? If they resonate with your vision, set up a few milestones that will help them get there.

In my case, I help online language teachers work smarter by moving away from the 1-on-1 lesson format. After that, I teach them how to create and sell more scalable options — programs and products.

I focus all of my work on the people who want that. But wanting alone doesn't get us there. Some of *my* community's milestones are: finding a niche and an ideal client, nailing the core message, dealing with fears and failure, and breaking mindset blocks that keep them from growing.

The milestones help me choose my content across different platforms. I repeat each concept multiple times in creative ways until I see that my audience engages with it. Then I move on to the next one. When I know what steps my client needs to take, finding creative ways to achieve the desired destination is easier. We can't expect people to *achieve* the vision just by resonating with it.

As leaders *we* decide *how to move our audience* from one point to the next in a doable way.

4. Invite others to enroll in the journey

From a business standpoint, the "journey" leads people from passive observers to paying clients. But our *leadership* doesn't end when we get money in our accounts. For me, an accomplished goal is also a changed mindset and a different lifestyle. I know that I've achieved my goal as a coach if a teacher hasn't just sold a product/service, but *changed in the process:* matured, resolved to persevere, learned to wait and help others.

That's why such an invitation is scary for your audience. It's easier to set a fake timer and force people topull out their credit card. But I guess if you're still reading this book, that isn't exactly your method.

When people *choose the journey* they commit to a deeper change, rather than some superficial image of it. That's why it's easier to eat watermelons to lose 20 pounds in one week (and then gain all that weight back) instead of **choosing a longer, more difficult path** of changing one's lifestyle.

This explains why the realistic timeline for achieving success as an online teacher and business owner is longer than a month, six months or even one year. Because not only is change itself hard, the process of *inspiring others to change* takes time.

Going back to the story I shared in the beginning, I believe **we are the leaders,** not just teachers for our online communities. I've discovered that people *are more enthusiastic* about following a vision rather than a set of expert tips. I'm not denouncing expertise, it has its place, but it makes sense only in the context of a bigger vision. By itself, expertise looks like a pile of random puzzle pieces that don't make one picture.

Carrie Anne James, the owner of French Is Beautiful, once said to me in an interview, "I like to get people to **fall in love with this universe that I've created.**"

She could have built a community of French learners and shared with them some tips on how to speak French without mistakes. Instead, she created a *universe* of *French lovers,* the incurable romantics, dreamy fashionistas and Parisian devotees who no doubt practice their French greetings while munching on a fresh croissant or a crunchy baguette.

With every one of her posts, Carrie Anne ignites that longing for Paris, her community's version of "the endless immensity of the sea." That is how you build a memorable brand.

So I want to inspire you to share your vision, not tips. Grow your tribe, not numbers. Lead your community to the vision you've created. They need **you** to help them achieve it; they can't do it on their own.

CHAPTER 13.
Finding the Strength to Keep Going

HEY THERE!

How's your week been? I'm about to share some fantastic content with you today — but there's a message I need to get off my chest first.

My personal mindset growth lesson for this week is...

Take the time to grieve your failure. This is where the magic begins.

I've been reading Brené Brown's "Rising Strong" (a book about the anatomy of failure), and boy has her message been a "spiritual awakening." (Find her TED talks on vulnerability and shame — you'll know what I'm alluding to).

So in my years of teacherpreneurship, one big lesson I've learned is... you can never run away from failing.

What that means is, at some point you will

- *launch a product that won't sell,*

- *work with clients who will not be satisfied,*

- *write a blog post/post a video that will generate poor comments,*

- *receive an email with complaints that you're overcharging.*

And that hurts.

I want it to sink in for a second.

It hurts. It hurts because we're creative human beings that are bringing value to others. We're risking everything when we hit that "publish" button and send that email. We're risking rejection.

And ... well ... failure happens. Don't sugarcoat it. Don't tell people, "I've made a mistake, but it's not a big deal." Don't pretend like it's not there.

Only those who never created anything significant can say that failing doesn't hurt. Because it does.

So acknowledge that it hurts. Grieve this loss. And then — you have a choice.

You can run away from it, or you can learn how to rise strong.

We all love safety and security. I talked to a budding teacherpreneur the other day who I can tell is so eager to create something unique but is scared it will fail, so she was asking me all these questions to make sure it was "safe to launch."

Safety and creativity don't go together. Safety wants to stay the same. Creativity wants to rock the boat. Change the world. Ignite people.

So it's not safe, but you know what?

I will do it anyway. Because I have opted out, and for me — there's no turning back. So I'll grieve my launch failures, my mistakes, the negativity of the people who have absolutely no idea what it's like to bring something unique into the world.

I will do it anyway.

I will do things differently. I will rock the boat. I will challenge the status quo.

Because I just can't imagine doing things any other way. Because I'm a teacherpreneur. And if you're reading this, and haven't unsubscribed, you are a teacherpreneur, too.

So create anyway. Be radical and rebellious. Rise strong.

. . .

"The opposite of recognizing that we're feeling something is denying our emotions. The opposite of being curious is disengaging. When we deny our stories

*and disengage from tough emotions, they
don't go away; instead, they own us, they
define us. Our job is not to deny the
story, but to defy the ending — to rise
strong, recognize our story, and rumble
with the truth until we get to a place
where we think, Yes. This is what
happened. This is my truth.
And I will choose how this story ends."*

— Brené Brown, "Rising Strong"

The email I quoted in the beginning was one of the most engaging pieces of writing I had done at that point. It immediately resonated with my audience, and they responded, sharing their stories of failures, telling me how much this email meant to them, adding they would print it out and post it over their desks.

Looking back over my years of running a business, I find the "big highlights" that everyone sees and envies are way less common than the steady "lowlights" that happen every day. Our "lowlights" are places of courage, resilience and perseverance — they teach us *how to keep going.*

In this chapter I want to share with you how I keep going when the lowlight season doesn't seem to end. When I think of myself as the slowest turtle, when I hesitate to get out of bed, when I doubt that people need what I have to offer, when the time and resources I put into a project outweigh the money that comes out of it...

1. I go back to my why

Why am I doing this, anyway? Just to pay my bills? This is why the "pick a niche in demand" advice doesn't work. It won't sustain you through the times when you can't pull yourself out of bed. For me, one of the reasons my core message of learning to work smarter exists is so I can help people go back to being more creative and passionate about the thing they love doing the most — teaching.

I do that because I feel most alive when I'm creative, and I know that they do, too. But when they stay busy with 1-on-1 lessons, passion and creativity go. This is **why** my work is important, this is why I do it and this is why I believe it will help many.

You would think that having one coaching session discussing my *why* is enough. No, I have to go back and rewrite it as often as I need so I don't get into the trap of, "Oh, so how can I make more money more easily? Maybe I should _____."

2. I ask myself what other options I have (and see if I like them)

When things are getting tough, my natural tendency is to quit what I'm doing and try out something else. My other options are: go find a real, 9-to-5 job (that will definitely "inspire" my creativity), start a new business or work on what I already have.

I realize that the process of looking for a 9-to-5 job is another full-time job, and if I'm really desperate I am skilled enough to do something part time (to which I prefer finding a "gig" like translating or writing). However, no matter how hard my lowlights have been I've never had to go down that route, and was able to wade through those temporary cash flow problems.

Starting a new business is worse than a 9-to-5 job or even fixing my current business. I could probably do things much faster from the strategic standpoint, but I know that it's best to work on what has already been established than to drop everything and come up with a new idea. And who has the time for that?

After I look at the options available, I remind myself that my best choice is to stick with what I have and to trust that things will work themselves out in the end. If nothing else I can read a book or journal or doodle or learn a language while I wait for people to respond to an offer in my newsletter.

3. I focus on keeping myself motivated (through reading and connecting)

How much of your day or week do you spend *intentionally* motivating yourself? We spend a lot of time working on websites, polishing offers, keeping up with social media, writing — doing all the important tasks we're supposed to do.

It struck me some time ago that motivation was never a part of my reading. I wouldn't intentionally take the time to think and write about resilience, passion or dedication to work. I would rather listen to a podcast that teaches me about the secrets of successful email campaigns than the one with some *motivational stories,* without flashy numbers or head-spinning business genius.

So I decided to immerse myself in the stories of people who have overcome, and spent time reflecting on how to develop those character traits that keep us going. I built connections with people who are doing the same kind of work that I do. Through reading, listening and spending time with people, I found a renewed inspiration for work, and I discovered that I was doubting and second-guessing myself less.

4. I remind myself how much I've done already

I've worked a lot to this point, and today I can say that I make a chunk of money while I sleep. As much as half of my operational expenses is covered by recurring revenue. Now you would think that a spoiled brat like that would be doing some wild celebration dance. Somehow that doesn't come as my first thought.

Instead (you guessed it), I stress over where *the other half* of my operational expenses is coming from, and why it takes *so long* to create enough recurring revenue to cover it. Sometimes I catch myself worrying about "the other half," my brain deep in the maze of new potential streams of revenue, clients and projects.

When that happens, I shock myself out of it, reminding myself how many hours I used to work to be where I am today. I train myself to appreciate these things that quickly become a norm, otherwise I'll be going back to "what still needs to be fixed" as opposed to "what I've already accomplished" — pat on the back.

5. I celebrate

Years ago when I was teaching five to seven lessons a day, and my new husband was working overtime to fundraise for a small nonprofit organization that did a lot of good, we established a tradition of coffee dates. I said with much authority and faith in my voice, "We will always have enough money for coffee." We've been going on coffee dates for the eight years of our marriage, dragging baby strollers, letting our kids crawl around on the floor, and now bargaining with them what drink is healthier.

Such small celebrations carry you through hard times and while they rarely break the bank, they boost your energy level and add excitement to your life as an online business owner. So when I get into a funk, I drive to a nearby coffee shop and order an extra-hot small cup of mocha. Then I look around and celebrate.

I celebrate having something I call *my own.* The little world where my work has helped people connect, create and thrive. The work that makes me alive, energized and more self-aware. The work that feels more like *art, fun and pleasure*. While it does have its many challenges and may not be a solution for everyone, I believe it suits who I am, what my values are and the direction I've set out for my life.

It's your turn now! If you feel stuck, go back to your *why* — write about it. Think of the people you've worked with, how much their lives have changed because of your work. Then look at your options and see if anything is as appealing as what you have right now. If something else has a strong pull on your heart, maybe you should pursue it.

Then, remind yourself how much you've already accomplished and give yourself a pat on the back. Your work matters, and it matters because of your consistency and perseverance.

Finally, go out and celebrate. Start your celebration tradition today. Get a coffee, an ice cream, a sushi plate — whatever feels like a celebration for you. The work you're doing today isn't going to be over soon, so you can choose how to feel about it and how to motivate yourself to persevere.

Conclusion

"The cliché of the anxious writer, pen frozen above a blank first page, never occurs to me. Instead, the blank page triggers wild anticipation. I'm on the edge of my seat, like an impatient child."

— Philippe Petit

IT'S BEEN SEVERAL YEARS since life took my business on a detour, and I tried to experiment with something that seemed impossible at the time. I wondered what would happen if I chose to work less. What would I have to change in order to be able to make the same income? How would these changes shape my life and work?

Sometimes we wait until "we're in a position" to do something different. We tend to feel deficient and somehow "not enough," we want to "get to that point" before we try for more. Perhaps this is the way things *should* work, but life doesn't always work the way it *should*.

I asked myself what I would do if I *had* the income I needed. My immediate response was, take time off, enjoy life, go on road trips, be present for my kids, read, create, focus on the meaning my work brings to others, not on the money it should deliver into my bank account. My next thought was, so why do I need to *wait* to get there? Why can I not do *some of it* now?

Thus began my journey into reducing my workload so I could focus on the things that mattered. I wanted to create a model that would free me to be more creative, and the more creative I became the more opportunities I found to increase my income, in a smart way.

I did it gradually: built my online community, turned some into clients, designed training programs to help them, hired two teammates, launched a membership program, quit the two-brand business to focus just on one, went from multiple launches a month to several launches a year.

Every single decision required a small step of faith, a lesson of patience and perseverance, a share of sacrifice and financial strain, and a reflection once the milestone was achieved. Every day I ask myself, "Is this a smart way of doing it? How can I do this task in less time? Do *I* have to do this task or can I hire someone else? Do I need *this task at all?*"

I want to inspire you to live the life you want to live **now.** Don't put it off until you make X amount, until you find another job, until your contract expires, until you have more time, until you find a way to fund your adventure 150%. Use common sense of course, but take a leap of faith **now.** And don't be afraid of challenges. **You can do hard things.**

Elena Mutonono

Acknowledgments

It takes a village to write a book. This book is no exception. From the time the concept entered my imagination until now, this book would not have seen the light of day in the form that I'd first envisioned if not for the support of my backers.

Thanks to the wonderful people below, I was able to polish up my writing, go through multiple drafts, hire a professional editor, an illustrator and a graphic designer. I've never put as much work into a book, and I'm thankful that my backers have made this project a reality, allowed me *not to cut corners* and pamper my perfectionism (just a little).

So big thanks to my multinational and multicultural fan team: Cara Leopold, Trisha Traughber, Tetiana Bilokin, Marta Piñero, Maria Seco, Elena Gabrielli, Kate Gregorio, Anastasiya Yildirim, Karina Thorne, Slobodan Kelečević, Veronika Palovska, Martina Scattolin, Curt Ford, Jevgenija Adamová, Ioana Elena Condrea, Yuriy Motin, Louise Robertson, David Gaffney, Mark Anderson, Alexandra Kapinya, Kate Fisher, Henneke Duistermaat, Ana Elisa Miranda, Dev Biswas, Bob Lejkowski-Clark, Michael Radparvar, Jeanne Ratzlaff, Danae Florou, Barbara Rocci, Kerstin Cable, Ines Ramos Perez, Paul Morgan, Laila Beidas, Linda Alley, Samantha Dematagoda, Kelly Nowocien, Natalia Melo, Clare Whitmell, Georges Carillet, Marie Sandi and the Creative Fund.

I appreciate my clients Elfin Waters and Fiona Young for letting me use their stories in this book.

I'm thankful to my online communities, the Opted Out group on Facebook and the Smart Teacher's Library — they provide ample inspiration and encouragement. They help me sharpen my core message and emphasize my *why*.

Special thanks to Trisha Traughber, my writing coach, for inspiring me to write creatively, struggle with the chapters that were tough to write, and graciously doing a final read-through to cross all the t's. Without you I would never have had the courage to edit my writing as thoroughly.

To Ioana Elena Condrea: Thank you for drawing such gorgeous flowers for the cover design.

To Veronika Palovska: Thank you for helping me make my brand beautiful, irresistible and memorable. Thank you for helping me raise the design bar as high as it should be. You've backed every one of my crazy ideas and stuck with me through thick and thin! Thank you for the gorgeous design you've created for this book and for my Kickstarter project. Thank you for being my friend and the sister I never had. Your work and your friendship have transformed my business and my life.

To Sondra Jackson: Thank you for joining my team; it's a dream that came true. Thank you (always) for helping me deal with overwhelm so efficiently. Thank you for loving and completing all the small tasks that I forget. Thank you for noticing the details. Thank you for all the memories we've shared, and the new ones we'll create. Thank you for giving me an excuse to take trips to Nashville "on business." You're a great friend and a Kindred Spirit.

I thank my parents for teaching me that anything is possible, that I can do hard things, and that life challenges should bring out the best in me.

Finally, I'm deeply grateful to my kids, Stephen and Vera, for teaching me that working smarter is the best gift I can give to them and to myself.

To Wimbai: Thank you for giving me a pair of wings.

Suggested Reading

Most quotes and concepts I refer to in this book come from the books I've read in the past. In case you want to add them to your reading list, here they are:

Anaejionu, Regina. *Be Small.* Blog post at www.byregina.com/be-small. 2016.

Brown, Brené. *Rising Strong: How the Ability to Reset Transforms the Way we Live, Love, Parent, and Lead.* New York, NY. Random House Trade Paperbacks, Reprint edition, 2017.

Craft, Kathryn. *The Art of Falling.* Naperville, IL. Sourcebooks Landmark, 2014.

Ephron, Delia. *Sister Mother Husband Dog: (Etc.)* New York, NY. Plume, 2013.

Erwin, Michael S. and Raymond Kethledge. *Lead Yourself First: Inspiring Leadership Through Solitude.* New York, NY. Bloomsbury USA, 2017.

Glibert, Elizabeth. *Big Magic: Creative Living Beyond Fear.* New York, NY. Riverhead Books, Reprint edition, 2016.

Godin, Seth. *Linchpin: Are You Indispensable?* New York, NY. Portfolio, 2010.

King, Stephen. *On Writing: A Memoir of the Craft.* New York, NY. Scribner, 2010.

Patel, Meera Lee. *My Friend Fear: Finding Magic in the Unknown.* New York, NY. TarcherPerigee, 2018.

Patel, Meera Lee. Start Where you Are: A Journal for Self-Exploration. New York, NY. TarcherPerigee, 2015.

Petit, Philippe. *Creativity: The Perfect Crime.* New York, NY. Riverhead Books, 2014.

Prince, Michelle. *Your Book Is Your Business Card.* McKinney, TX. Performance Publishing Group, 2017.

Tharp, Twyla. *The Creative Habit: Learn and Use It for Life.* New York, NY. Simon & Schuster, Reprint edition, 2006.

Wood, David. *What Have We Done: The Moral Injury of Our Longest Wars.* Boston, MA. Little, Brown and Company, 2016.

About the author

ELENA MUTONONO has been teaching online since 2008, trying out Skype lessons and buggy beta webinar software that few people in her home country of Ukraine knew how to use. In 2009, she received a grant from the Regional English Language Office at the U.S. Embassy in Kyiv, Ukraine, to develop online training programs for schoolteachers.

After several years of teaching 1-on-1, Elena began experimenting with different online business models that would allow online teachers to scale their businesses much faster while doing the things they loved and impacting more people with their messages of change.

Her focus now is smart online teaching that helps teachers and coaches gain more creative and financial freedom.

You can find Elena at elenamutonono.com.

Notes

* The names marked with an asterisk have been changed to protect the privacy of individuals.

i Source: https://www.ptsd.va.gov/professional/treat/cooccurring/moral_injury.asp

ii Source: https://www.etymonline.com/word/forgive

iii www.mnibconsulting.com

v There are, of course, other problems, such as poorly defined niche (specifically, no niche, or niche chosen for its perceived value for the market), little understanding of one's audience, no consistent content creation (and a low trust level with your clients as a result), content that adds to the noise but doesn't create tension (note all the "tips" videos and blog posts), lack of strategic vision and no understanding of one's core message. If you're not clear on your strategy, content, client, core message or niche, creating a product won't add to sales.

vi As a side note here: It's not impossible to sell higher-price products following a free demo, but the success of such a model depends on the audience. I'm speaking of my own teaching/coaching experience and relating the No. 1 struggle of my clients. But the model can be different for people working in other areas or selling to businesses.

vii www.doyouspeakfreedom.com